"Vivian Shapiro has gif... inspirational. Her joie de vi... for readers to question, confirm and challenge the traits that support or constrain their efforts to live life fully."

JUDITH SEIGEL

Ph.D., LCSW Author of "What Children Learn from Their Parent's Marriage" and "Stop Overreacting: Effective Strategies for Calming your Emotions."

"Vivian's book takes me to a high frequency that I intend to live at more often. Her words are powerful, potent, and filled with magic. Vivian is one of the most incredible humans I have ever met, and her book exuberates the essence of who she is. I can't recommend reading her book highly enough if you would like to learn how to become more vibrant in your own life. Vivian's poetry is a gift for your soul."

KATIE CAREY

CEO Katie Carey Media LTD | 5 x Amazon No.1 International Best-Selling Author International Best-Selling Publisher | Top 0.5% global ranked podcast host at Soulfulvalley Podcast | Poet | Intuitive Business & Manifestation Coach/Mentor

Go Vibrant!

... notes & anecdotes
on loving and living
the joie de VIVre

Vivian Shapiro

GO VIBRANT!
 … notes & anecdotes on loving and living the joie de VIVre
 © Copyright 2023 Vivian Shapiro

All rights reserved. No part of this publication may be reproduced, distributed or transmitted in any form or by any means, including photocopying, recording, or other electronic or mechanical methods, without the prior written permission of the publisher, except in the case of brief quotations embodied in critical reviews and certain other noncommercial uses permitted by copyright law.

Although the author and publisher have made every effort to ensure that the information in this book was correct at press time, the author and publisher do not assume and hereby disclaim any liability to any party for any loss, damage, or disruption caused by errors or omissions, whether such errors or omissions result from negligence, accident, or any other cause.

Adherence to all applicable laws and regulations, including international, federal, state and local governing professional licensing, business practices, advertising, and all other aspects of doing business in the US, Canada or any other jurisdiction is the sole responsibility of the reader and consumer.

Neither the author nor the publisher assumes any responsibility or liability whatsoever on behalf of the consumer or reader of this material. Any perceived slight of any individual or organization is purely unintentional.

The resources in this book are provided for informational purposes only and should not be used to replace the specialized training and professional judgment of a health care or mental health care professional.

Neither the author nor the publisher can be held responsible for the use of the information provided within this book. Please always consult a trained professional before making any decision regarding treatment of yourself or others.

For more information, email vivianshapiro@rogers.com
ISBN: (paperback) 979-8-88759-521-4
ISBN: (ebook) 979-8-88759-522-1

Get Your Free Gift!

DOWNLOAD YOUR PERSONAL JOURNAL FREE!

Hey readers!

Thank you so much for purchasing the kindle or paperback version of **GO VIBRANT!** To say thanks, I would like to gift you with this companion!

I know you are more likely to participate in the exercises and get the best interactive experience when, instead of writing in the book itself, you download your own:

HEY VIBRANT YOU! IT'S YOUR TURN.
Personal Vibrancy Journal

GET THE FREE COPY OF YOUR JOURNAL NOW BY VISITING:

vivianshapiro.com/journal

Dedication

*I dedicate this book to my supportive life partner, Rowland
and all our combined adult children
who have bestowed on us
the wonderful gift
of a plethora of beautiful grandchildren
who keep me striving to maintain vibrancy
and for whom I hope to instil
my joie de **VIV**re*

*A special thanks goes to
my biological sons
Jody and Todd Shapiro
who playfully tease me
with words that say
I am an **ACE!**
that is …*
A *Annoying*
C *Crazy*
E *Embarrassing*

(all in jest of course)

*My hope is that when they read this book,
maybe they will understand why!*

Contents

GO VIBRANT!

notes & anecdotes on loving and living the joie de VIVre

Introduction 13

Chapter 1: Free to Be Vibrant Me 31

Chapter 2: Star One: VIVA LA Vs 41
      Creating your Vibration, Living Values & more

Chapter 3: Star Two: INVITING THE Is 59
      I am, Imagine, Interests, Interested, Interesting,
      Intentions, Inspired, Inspire, Integrity & more

Chapter 4: Star Three: SO B IT!. 93
      Bold, Be, Brave, Believe, Bodacious & more

Chapter 5: Star Four: ROAR THOSE Rs! 117
      Roar, Recharge, Routines & Rituals, Resilience,
      Radiance, Reflection, Rose Coloured Glasses & more

Chapter 6: Star Five : Ace the As 141
      Action, Adventure, Achievements, Audacious,
      Abundance, Attitude of Gratitude & more

Chapter 7:   Star Six: Start with the N Game in Mind 177
             Nurture, Nourish, say No, Nature, Nirvana,
             Naughty, Nice & Nuts Practices of Finding Nurviva

Chapter 8:   Star Seven: Fits You to a T .199
             Tenacity, Tribe, Tenderness, Team, Togetherness,
             Truth, Thankfulness

Chapter 9:   Life is Like a Box of Analogies 241

Chapter 10: Not The End 255

I HAD A VISION

I had a vision
that Vibrance came to me
and this is what she whispered in my ear:

"I am Vibrance.
Who am I?
I am one and I am many
ignited by flames of visions
Of visualizations
Of verve and vitality
Loving to dance and frolic
in the colours of life,
I breathe in intensity
I breathe out passion.
I'm authentically alive!
I live with and through
both pain and pleasure.
In the playgrounds of positivity,
I sensually seize each day.
I will refresh you…
Help you feel resilient
Help you feel alive with
love
life
light
and
laughter.
I offer invitations
to all
to drink a full glass
of my sweet sensation.
Stir it soulfully
so you may be fulfilled
by its magical secrets"

(Fortunately, I listened well!)
Vivian Shapiro - Jan. 2022

INTRODUCTION
WELCOME TO MY WORLD!

This book comes to you via my vivid long term memory (so much better than my short one!) along with my 40+ years of journal writing, those notebooks being the true sources for this endeavour of mine. But why write a book?

When things are meant to be…

There it was yet again. That phrase: *"I want to be you when I grow up!"* followed by the question, *"Viv, how do you do it? Where do you get that energy and how do you stay so vibrant?"* I was reconnecting with a friend and teacher that I had hired and had not seen for over fifteen years. After engaging in a very lively discussion, Robyn looked into my eyes and added, *"No really, Viv! I want to know. What is your secret sauce?"* Of course, I was flattered.

It's been something I have heard many times, since I was maybe 45, and fortunately at 76 at the time of this writing, I am still hearing it. This time was different. I didn't just slough it off, giggle and thank the person modestly. I stated determinedly and boldly (and quite loudly I might add), *"I am going to find out!"* I think my friend thought I had truly lost my mind.

That evening, I went into a deep and serious self-study. I needed to find out the answers to my questions:

- "Why do people say that to me?"
- "Who was I?"
- "What was I still meant to do?

I created a list of the most common phrases that come my way and I am proud to share these with you!

- *I wanna be you when I grow up!*
- *I wish I had your energy.*
- *You pick me up.*
- *I'm inspired by watching you.*
- *How do you always see the strengths in even those who have treated you wrongly?*
- *You always manage to have a positive attitude!*
- *You light up a room.*
- *I love how you always come up with solutions.*
- *You are the eternal optimist.*
- *You saved my life!*
- *You remind me of Goldie Hawn!*

Yes, all of these are indeed very flattering and quite lovely. What is it that I did or continue to do to deserve such high praise and recognition? What exactly is it that I do or have done to live with a positive, forward moving mindset? How have I lived my life to present myself as this person others want to emulate?

Other than weakly acknowledging my strengths, I have allowed my eyes to focus on my weaknesses. I have succumbed to my own view of myself as insecure, needy, self-deprecating, compulsive, definitely type A, a perfectionist, sometimes controlling, and even a bit bitchy. As well I know that I can be too much for people, much too much. Jealousy and intimidation have led envious colleagues and acquaintances to bully me or create untrue rumours about me!

INTRODUCTION

Thank goodness that's a small percentage. Their loss. They missed out having a true loyal, fun-loving and supportive friend that would go to the ends of the earth for them!

Many friends, family and acquaintances have tried to open my eyes to those aspects that humble me, fill my heart with love and make me realize I have "some 'splaining to do", as Ricky would often say to Lucy! I was now ready to honour me and explain proudly.

I was up for the task; I was ready to plunge into the core of me to discover what I was truly all about. What were the characteristics, the attributes that made me stand out as *Vibrant* to others? What was my secret sauce? Correction: What IS my secret sauce?

These questions propelled me to enter the doorway to my stash of over forty journals. Started over 40 years ago, their covers have more colours than Joseph's coat!

My journals are my best friends. They allow me to say or tell stories about anything! They don't judge, they do not receive marks for literary prowess, and best of all they don't answer back! (Although sometimes I answer myself back!)

Writing in a journal, for me, for many years, was how I made promises to myself, where I allowed my deepest thoughts and feelings to erupt with no real intention other than perhaps to release them. I presumed that I would eventually look back and see if I did indeed do what I hoped to achieve or advised myself to do. But up until now, I had not revisited these treasures.

Different from my pre-teen and teenage journals containing gossip and information on my latest crushes or BFF adventures, writing in my adult journals was a way for me to bring my adventures to life, make honest comments about events, and to bring my artistic skills to the fore, especially that of my poetic self. Truthfully and sadly, I had not spent much time checking in with my past self that was speaking to my future self. However, my journal writing continues to this day, albeit in many changed formats. The good news? I saved them ALL! I decided it was now time to dedicate myself to pouring myself into my words and reliving my truths.

I couldn't wait to venture down the multicoloured road of "Journal Land" to find my VIBRANT SELF and discover the MAGIC of ME! (And whatever other things I would uncover.) Gleefully, I went on this journey with my highlighters, sticky notes and my backpack full of additional questions:

- *Have I learned from past experiences?*
- *Had I met my intended goals?*
- *Had I followed up on promises I made to myself?*
- *Had I listened to my own advice?*

Perhaps there was more of a purpose to these forty-plus notebooks of various sizes and shapes than to take up a special IKEA unit that housed them along with my many photo albums. Perhaps I could find something worth sharing with the world. Perhaps there was a gift in the many words and thoughts poured into these pages that might help someone find their truer self. I was about to find out. First the purpose was to find my true self!

When looking at yourself through objective eyes…

Before me lay a combination of tender, heartbreaking, happy, angry, sensitive stories of every kind of genre and subject; my own personal thoughts on living, learning, loving, in a variety of forms; beautiful, sad, angry, funny excerpts; clever poems, both rhyming and free verse; ideas for songs; rough drafts of songs that actually made it on Billboard; Vivianisms (my unique sayings); sketches; drawings;

favourite lines from songs; personal paintings, and portraits when the mood struck me.

I was stunned when I read through them. I was surprisingly impressed at my writing ability and sensitivity. My words, even to this day as I continue to write, are written without thought to grammar, spelling, meaning but just flow. As I dove deep into my journals, keeping my modesty in my back pocket, I congratulated myself on how perceptive and enlightening I sounded!

I did find a number of qualities of mine that did stand out no matter the content, my family's or life's crazy moments, my exuberant or my angry bitter experiences. I realized I could fill up the letters of VIBRANT to create an acronym, and oh how I love acronyms!

Throughout many of my stumbling blocks and challenges, whether they were family, relationship, health-based or other, I found out, no matter what, even past the lowest moments and deepest of funks, I focused on remaining…

V *a Visionary with Vitality*

I *an Inspirer and Influencer*

B *a Bold Bossbabe*

R *a Resilient and Radiant force*

A *an Action-oriented Achiever*

N *a Nurturing soul, searching her own Nirvana*

T *a Tenacious Trailblazer Thankful for her Tribe*

I was VIBRANT with experiences full of love, losses and lessons! That's when the book that I was meant to write appeared to me in a vision! The timing was perfect.

When a vision becomes clear…

At the very moment that I was actually contemplating having something to offer others, revealing my secret sauce while leaving a legacy for my family, I was contacted by a self-publishing school to take a look at their courses and coaching. *How did they know? The universe!* After receiving a 45-minute free workshop on the possibilities, I realized that this publishing school and my learning modality were a match! The support, coaching and lessons offered to a newbie author aligned with what I was looking for. This was the Law of Attraction in action!

I envisioned a book that would capture my joie de vivre, (actually my "joie de **VIV**-re!") capitalizing on my name and a potpourri of my adventures and stories in no necessarily chronological order that would depict a life of VIBRANCY, of verve and vitality no matter the circumstances. I imagined my purpose and my intention would be to make the most of who and what I was to serve myself, my family and my community to the best of my ability. I now had answers and stories I was ready to share. I knew these stories would be strictly from my own truths and perspectives and perhaps others would have different versions. Nonetheless, I believed I had a mission to share my experiences as I myself had lived them.

I had fun creating in my head many titles that would capture a book on Living a VIBRANT Life and was excited about this one:

Go Vibrant !
notes and anecdotes on living and loving the "joie de VIVre"

I envisioned the chapters named after each of the letters in VIBRANT and as I did so, more words with each of those beginning letters beckoned to be mentioned. I was uncovering the secret sauce within myself that gave credence and life to those descriptive words.

INTRODUCTION

They addressed the questions people had been asking of me. I now had answers I was ready to share!

And thus a potential book and a new budding author was born, labour pains and all. I had many moments of imposter syndrome, wondering *"Who am I to write a book to tell others how to live?"*

I then realized I was not "telling others" anything.

I remembered McDonalds' claim to fame in the 70's was their Big Mac with a clever tongue twisting jingle: *"two all beef patties, special sauce, lettuce, cheese, pickles, onions and a sesame seed bun"*. The jingle hit the airwaves and everyone was singing it, or attempting to have success with this catchy rap. Today we would declare that it went viral! It was the customer's choice however whether to engage in the whole experience. Some may wish to devour it as suggested, while others may try it with only a few of the ingredients. I envisioned that I too could offer my special sauce ingredients with an invitation to bite into my vibrant hamburger. It would be the readers' choice whether to top it up with all the fixings! This was not about "telling", this was about "sharing".

When reading through my chapters…

The experiences and stories are mine, authentic and remembered, shared with the intention to align with those characteristics I saw as keeping me living a full vibrant life. Certainly there were times when my vibrancy was low and like anyone else I would get in a funk, sometimes for months, so please know I'm not always "Pollyanna Perky Pat!" When that occurred I learned ways to bring me back to my joyous self through healing, practitioners, coaches, authors, yoga teachers, fitness trainers, meditation, friends and family as well as scribing time in my journals.

A good teacher learns from the teachers who influenced them. The added suggestions given in this book, along with my personal adventures, are a combination of the incredible strategies, words and teachings I absorbed from all of the sources above. I am truly grateful and continue to be grateful for those out there that share their gifts with others.

The AFFIRMATIONS pages are yours to explore and see which personal messages to yourself will fit for you. Choose which ones have meaning for you. Say them out loud! By all means add your own!

The "HEY VIBRANT YOU! workbook sections" come from me and my many years of teaching. *"Oh there she goes again, Vivian/mom/my wife doing her "teaching thing!"* was a commonly heard phrase. And here I am again doing my teacher thing. I first chastised myself by wondering *"Who am I to assume the role of teacher here?"* but my vibrant side retorted, *"And who are you not to!"*

I love writing in books, in margins, and highlighting. I appreciate guided questions and workspace. The teacher in me has given you these along with some exercises or activities in order to be able to align yourself to the messages in each chapter. Enjoy the challenges set before you. Whether on Kindle or reading via paperback, make your own VIBRANT journal to personalize your reading experience. Please know these "HEY" sections are purposefully randomly placed. Enjoy the variety!

BONUS! If you have purchased the book, you will notice that you can print and make your own booklet of the "HEY VIBRANT YOU exercises" for free simply by using this QR Code.

INTRODUCTION

Here for you now, is your first one to get you started! Yes, in the introduction no less!

HEY VIBRANT YOU! IT'S YOUR TURN.
The Name Game

> 'Tis but thy name that is my enemy;
> Thou art thyself, though not a Montague.
> What's Montague? It is nor hand, nor foot,
> Nor arm, nor face, nor any other part
> Belonging to a man. O, be some other name!
> **What's in a name? That which we call a rose**
> **By any other name would smell as sweet;**
> So Romeo would, were he not Romeo call'd,
> Retain that dear perfection which he owes
> Without that title. Romeo, doff thy name,
> And for that name which is no part of thee
> Take all myself
> - William Shakespeare, Romeo and Juliet

What's in our names? Let's get acquainted and be friends!

Hi! I am Vivian! What's your name?

It is amazing what a simple introduction, used often by kids, can do to start a whole new relationship. You and I will be having a relationship, so let's start with proper introductions!

I am Vivian Shapiro, born Viviana Tauba Ader Leinung, but more on the birth name later!

What's your name? What's your full birth name?

No, really! What's your name? Write it down here.

If you are reading online, or on Kindle, I invite you to use the workbook available on my website or find a journaling notebook to use while reading. I invite you to do so before you begin! (And make sure you use a great flowing type of pen…it's all about the pen!)

Let's start again:

Hi! I am Vivian. What's your name?
Answer here:

_____

Me: "Nice to meet you!"

Choosing our name…

We really have no influence on the name bestowed upon us. Other people, usually our parents, choose it for us, usually after many days of slow and long deliberations, revisiting names of past family members, or finding unique names, some that may remind one of a memory or times in nature or the season. And without so much as a frown or smile or word in edgewise, we take on our name for our lifetime. (Unless we change it later!)

I was born Viviana Tauba Ader Leinung in Lisbon, Portugal on November 20 1945.

My mother was enamoured with the movie star Vivien Leigh from *Gone With the Wind* and thus my name, only written as a Portuguese derivation. I have no idea where Tauba came from. I think they needed a middle name that started with a T and came up with

INTRODUCTION

that. When I was young, my mother told me it meant "little doe" in German and all these years, I thought that was so sweet until I found out, just now, it means "pigeon". Maybe I cooed a lot? The Ader was my mother's maiden name. Leinung is, of course, my family name. All in all, not a particularly attractive name.

When I came through immigration in New York, one very very cold snowy day in December in 1947, they changed my first name from Viviana to Vivian. Go figure! Tauba stayed the same! I will never understand that.

From a very young age I was not a fan of my name. In fact I hated it. I hated Vivian. I hated Tauba. And my last name? No-one could pronounce it. It was thought to be LEE NUNG when it really was pronounced LIE NOONG. Teachers who saw my name on their new class list assumed I would be Asian. And told me so.

Everyone else was either Sandra, Jane, Susan, Kathy or lovely double names like Mary Catherine. Even my sister, born years later, was named Karen Ann! So sweet! In high school, Grade 9, I changed my middle name to Tobey after reading books from the 1950s Tobey Heydon series, *Practically Seventeen*. I asked all my friends and teachers to start calling me that name. That lasted 3 months until my mom had an interview with the teacher who kept talking about a student named Tobey and my mom thought she was in the wrong room!

My mom could not understand how I could NOT love the beautiful name Viviana (or now Canadianized to Vivian!) and told me I would grow to love it. She told me it was "perfect" for me. In fact, my mom and dad were right on the mark. How could she have known it would end up being so? It took a while, but eventually I saw that it was indeed a name that really suited my personality, joy of life and mission in life.

Growing to love my name…

I now do indeed love the name and all its derivatives that I have been called. *Vibrant Viv, Vivacious Viv, Viva (my signature on my art work), Viv, Vivi, Vivichen (an endearing term used by my mom and dad, basically meaning dear Vivi), Vivitar, (coined by my friend Lorne) Vava, (all my 13 grand-kiddies call me that!), Vivienne to all my French friends (how I love the sound of that!) and Viviana (my original passport name that I now love to use, when I travel in Europe or Mexico)*

I found out so much about my name on the internet. Too bad Google was not around when I was a child! From a plethora of google searches, I found out:

- *Vivian is derived from the Latin vivus, meaning alive.*
- *Vivian Name Origin: Latin*
- *Pronunciation: viv-ee-in*
- *Originally a male name, little Vivian has mostly left the unisex space stateside to become a solidly female choice as seen in movies.*
- *Vivian does have tons of alternative spellings to contend with, including Vivienne, Viviane, and Vivien, though Vivian tends to be the most commonly used.*
- *It's a timeless classic name bursting with style and elegance.*
- *It's fashionable and regal on an adult, but can be lightened up as Viv or Vivi on a little one.*

And when you do research on Personality Traits, apparently Vivian…

- *loves the excitement of life.*
- *can easily adapt to all situations.*
- *thrives on the new and unexpected.*
- *prefers to be in constant motion so they feel alive.*

INTRODUCTION

- *will stir up some action if there's not enough around.*
- *is an inherent risk-taker, pushing the envelope.*
- *is naturally rebellious.*
- *has no fear and never resists change.*
- *loves travelling and new experiences.*
- *is very social and attracts friends with ease.*
- *is optimistic and good-natured.*
- *has a quick wit, a cerebral mind, and is generally very persuasive.*
- *is freedom-loving, adventurous, adaptable, intellectual, easygoing, progressive*
- *and sensual.*

Seriously! With the exception of *easy-going*, how did my parents know that along with my true Scorpio personality (which I will not go into now), I am so much like most of the comments made fit for a "Vivian".

My favourite characters in movies/books are Miss Vivian played by Julia Roberts from *Pretty Woman* and the character of Vivian Walker from *Divine Secrets of the Ya-Ya Sisterhood!*

And there you have it! I love my name and continue to try to honour it!

And is it coincidental that I have made super good friends with two lovely ladies, Vivien Cord and Vivian Singh, both who have come into my life through a chance meeting! Meant to be!

Go Vibrant!

HEY VIBRANT YOU! IT'S YOUR TURN.
Name It!

Print your birth name in a very artistic way, worthy of your name. Dress it up!

If you changed it from birth, or it changed via circumstance, print your name as you like to be called:

Do you like your name? Why or Why not?

_____
_____
_____
_____
_____
_____

How has your opinion of your name changed over the years?

_____
_____
_____
_____
_____

INTRODUCTION

If you could change it, what would you change it to?

_____
_____
_____
_____
_____
_____

If you haven't already, do a google search on your name. What have you found out? Are you a match?

_____
_____
_____
_____
_____
_____

Play with your name. Play with your signatures or your initials. Make your name come alive. Make it you! Create a number of signatures or logos. Circle which you like best.

My intention for writing this book…

Other than to create and achieve something in my lifetime of which I personally could be proud, I intend to leave a legacy for my adult children and grandchildren (and maybe even a great-grandchild). I hope I will give them an insight into who I was and why I was who I was, did what I did and lived how I lived. My hope is that they will find or take one idea for themselves to help them live a VIBRANT life.

And for you, my readers? I do not profess to be an advisor, a coach, a psychiatrist, a preacher, a social worker, a healer, a therapist or a celebrity writing their memoirs. What I am is a lover of life, an observer of opportunities, a scriber of stories, an editor of experiences, a singer of songs, a ponderer of poetry, an empath of everything, a feeler of fantasies, a masseuse of messages, a teacher of thoughts, a dealer of dreams.

I am, in fact, just like you. I am just an ordinary person with ordinary experiences, yet extraordinary messages that may help one find strategies for a happier, more joyful, engaging and truer you, living a life you control, a life in which you will be empowered to rise above, no matter the entanglements.

My invitation…

I encourage you to join me through my adventures, messages, creative activities and personal responses to your own questions, to step out of your comfort zone. I hope this book makes you laugh with me, cry with me, hurt for me, feel joy for me, relate to me, create with me, see parts of yourself in me, and reflect along with me.

More importantly, for you, I hope this book helps you cry for you, hurt for you, feel joy for you, relate to you, create for you, see yourself in you, love yourself and go out with purpose to live a full and vibrant life with intention, kindness and happiness. And pay it forward.

Why would you want to live vibrantly? I invite you to read the book and find out!

Lokah Samastah Sukhino Bhavantu
is a Sanskrit mantra to radiate the feeling of love and happiness towards the world.

*"May all beings everywhere be happy and free,
and may the thoughts, words, and actions of my own life
contribute in some way
to that happiness and to that freedom for all."*

THANK YOU ALL.
YOU ARE BEAUTIFUL AND LOVED AND VIBRANT!

CHAPTER 1
Free to Be Vibrant Me

When you have to make a difficult decision…

I ran into the house, locked the door and shed the tears welling deep inside of me. I was a mess. I knew what I had to do! It was time. But first I needed someone to lean on.

I called my girlfriend at midnight, but when she picked up the phone I could barely speak. Without hesitation, she said, "It sounds like you could use some emotional support." As a true good friend is bound to do, she met me at Tim Hortons, her pajamas still on underneath her spring jacket. We sipped on our steaming coffee as she helped me unload my hurting heart. May 26, 1994, will be forever etched in my mind as the day I unlocked my cage. Sharon B. sat and listened compassionately as I spoke. It is amazing that she even understood me as the words were muffled by heavy sobs, tears flowing down my reddened eyes.

Earlier that day, I had been looking forward to our Annual Principals' Dinner Dance Event. Sharon and I were going together without spouses. Mine was at a nearby conference and unavailable and hers disliked that sort of thing. Fine! We were a great bonded, congenial group of colleagues who knew how to work hard and play hard, and though spouses and partners were definitely invited and included, a few colleagues chose to come solo.

My husband changed his mind at the last minute, calling to say he had decided to come home to attend with me. I really was not sure why this sudden change of mind, as he was adamant the day before that he could not and would not be there! With this news, Sharon decided to stay home. I pretended I was thrilled at this sudden change; however, something was telling me to say "No, don't come!" What was that line from *Pretty Woman* that Miss Vivian said to the high fashion store clerks? "BIG MISTAKE… BIG! HUGE!" Yes Miss Viv! "BIG MISTAKE!" I should have listened to my instincts. But then the rest would not have happened. And it was meant to.

The event itself was fabulous but for me it was a disaster. The evening became a battleground for what was already a dysfunctional relationship. My husband was angry for whatever reasons unbeknownst to me. I was blamed for choosing to sit with colleagues of mine that talked shop and for a host of other reasons as to why he thought I was not a good wife. We usually looked like a happy, well-balanced couple on the dance floor and that is where I led him. I assumed that emotions would fade away while we danced…they did not.

In a louder than normal voice, many accusatory hurtful words were said to me, right in the middle of the dance floor. I could see by the look of pity in the eyes of one of my colleagues dancing nearby how sad she was for me. I excused myself and went to the bathroom in an attempt to regain my composure. My friend who witnessed my unhappiness came to see how I was, hugged me, and said, "Oh Vivian, you of all people don't deserve that!" This was my final WAKE UP call! And I answered, "Thank you, Bev. You are absolutely right!"

I asked her if she wouldn't mind going into the event area to tell my husband that I was waiting in the car to go home. As I gathered

FREE TO BE VIBRANT ME

my things from the dinner table to make my quiet departure, I felt others' quizzical eyes on me, wondering why their lively, social, "dance-til-the-music-stops" colleague was retiring so early. I couldn't even look at anybody. The pain of embarrassment was too great.

When he opened the car door, I had already detached myself. Thus, this driver of the car was given cool, unemotional instructions to take me straight home and to go back to his %#@## Conference if he wished. Somehow in that moment, I grew strong. Despite my insides being torn asunder, my mind was clear and calm, full of courage and conviction.

At the coffee shop later, Sharon offered me the strength I needed to pause, breathe and reflect. I confessed that I could not take the hurt anymore. She acknowledged my pain and affirmed my value as a person. It may seem like a small incident, but it was unfortunately one of too many occurrences of our declining marriage. I was done. I felt unappreciated and undervalued. Though once again, my heart was broken, my vision was suddenly fixed! No one could define my worth but me. Here I was after many unhappy years, ready to get out of this pattern of concession and set myself free. I would emerge from my cocoon as the beautiful vibrant butterfly I knew I could be, ready to spread my wings. I was beckoned to fly higher into a better space.

I slept well that night, prepared for what I knew my decision would be the next day. I was prepared to step into my power and reclaim responsibility for my happiness! Until…I woke up with Debbie Doubt lying right beside me! She entered my mind and soul and I immediately jumped into my "insecurity" role. Feeling guilty about not having had more compassion or support for my husband surrounded by my colleagues and all their "shop talk," I decided to apologize and left him a message at his office to call me. We were married for 28 years, a lot to give up! Yes, I was running around that familiar track yet again, still hoping for things to change along the way.

However, it was no coincidence that as soon as I drove out of the driveway for work, the radio was blaring the lyrics of "I Will Survive" by Gloria Gaynor. These lyrics spoke to me loud and clear:

"It took all the strength I had not to fall apart
Kept trying hard to mend the pieces of my broken heart
And I spent oh-so many nights just feeling sorry for myself
I used to cry, but now I hold my head up high
And you see me, somebody new,
I'm not that chained up little person still in love with you…"

And I knew that I too would survive! I needed to forget how I felt and remember what I deserved. My heart was finally accepting what my mind already knew. By the end of the song, my mind was made up. I was running my victory lap, the last one and getting prepared for the celebration ahead. Debbie Doubt had left the building for good!

At 11AM his call was put through to my principal's office. I simply said, "I want you to know, I'm calling a mediator recommended to me. I will see you at home. I have to go, I'm busy." And that was the beginning of the end and a start to the new and improved me.

As sad as I was, I felt a great weight being lifted from my mind, body and soul. I saw it as a new chapter for me! What would I call this new life? I quickly wrote in my journal what this chapter might be called in my imaginary book:

Free to be Vibrant Me
Goodbye at Last
Feeling Elated
Relieved and Rejuvenated
A Heavy Burden Lightened
Flying Higher
Empowered to Be Me
It's a New Start
Energized
Lightening My Load
Feeling Empowered
Unentangled

I knew it would not be easy, but one thing I knew was I was staying true to myself, honouring me!

Here is the poem I wrote two days later:

FINDING VIVIAN

Freedom at last
A break from the past
No more words that rip apart
No surging pain upon my heart

The truth was told
A decision bold
Made clear with fear and trepidation
Yet what I feel is pure elation

No more questions no accusing
No more hurtful word-abusing
Free oh yes so free am I
Should I feel this good, this high?

> *I know I'll come down very soon*
> *Amidst the family life now ruined*
> *I only hope that what I have done*
> *Will leave no damage to my sons*
>
> *I'm ready to take my new life on*
> *Living alone now where I belong*
> *Finding myself, being true to me*
> *I'm free, I'm free My God … I'm free*

Vivian Shapiro - May 1994

May 28, 1994. The start of a new day, a new life. I admit I was terrified.

When seeking help fails…

I honestly don't know what happened in the 28 years together, but we did not work any more. Our relationship was more than dysfunctional. It was sad…very sad, because I believe that we really did love each other.

Life wasn't always maladaptive. We were a very handsome couple in the late 1960s and onward for quite a few years. We were very social, adventurous, adoring each other, proud and loving parents of two delicious boys who were an absolute treat. We were travellers, homeowners, cottage owners, ambitious in our own fields of work, successful, music lovers, car fanatics, concert goers, jive dance contest winners, and the list goes on. But we were both unhappy.

We did try therapy before this. They say if even a small ember exists in that heap of wood, which might ignite by fanning it, you should try to see if the fire can be restarted. Our therapist stated: "You two are like a golden Cadillac. You look good, all stylish and classy, but when you open the hood the motor doesn't work!" (If it were today, he'd call it a Tesla with no charger!) I personally think it was so broken, it likely would not even be picked up for a used car lot! Ready for the junkyard it was.

Therapy only helps when there are no lies told. Therapy only helps when each person is careful to not manipulate the conversation. Therapy only helps when each person plays authentically and is willing to see their own areas for improvement. Therapy only helps when you truly madly deeply want things to change. Therapy is not about blaming; it is about finding ways together that will aid in repairing, restoring, and renewing, writing a clean slate based on love and respect. Our motor was beyond repair, ego was our fuel and thus the guidelines were not always adhered to.

We separated very soon after the dinner dance evening and both our lives took on a whole new chapter in two vastly different books. The next two years were brutal for me. I became easily depressed when alone and found myself in "no person's land", an island unto myself. I was fortunate to have very supportive staff, friends and a close family. I did remain true to my promise to look after myself and shine my worth once more!

When you recognize you have a gift…

This book is a slice of my soul, not in any chronological order. There are lessons learned from the stories in my journals that I have been writing since I was 35 years old! My promise to myself after our separation was to live a full, blessed, treasured life where I valued not only my family and friends but through consistent and conscious intention, I would live a vibrant full-on life.

I had a gift and I was unwrapping it slowly. This gift presented itself often to my close friends and work colleagues, yet unfortunately was a gift that, in the presence of my husband, was left tightly wrapped up in a dark closet, seeing the light only in his absence. I vowed to never leave it lonely and unwanted again.

What was in my package? One of the items was my inherent character of positivity. Through my most hurting times, I allowed my positivity to break down the "tough times" or "poor me" wall. I focused on my gift. I centred my thoughts on the fact that my husband and I had lots of good years and brought into this life two very amazing now-adult males with many talents and abilities to offer the world.

Although my gift was not appreciated by my spouse, perhaps there were other gifts elsewhere that would suit him better in his new life. He could find a new car with a motor that worked with his chassis. Me too. While I wasn't in any rush at all to look for that new car with a humming motor, I knew, in time, there would be one special edition out there. It was probably in the used car lot, given up by an unappreciative owner, but one that would suit my style, with a driver that would adore me as the co-driver. (Turns out there was!)

During my early years of separation, I started to realize bit by bit the gift I had to pass on to others. First I worked on rising above my own hurt and my worry about being alone. I tried to remain unplugged and started to listen to only affirming and acknowledging words. My aperture opened. I vowed to make better choices. Where focus goes, energy flows. My focus would be intentional. I would not allow myself to get entangled in anyone else's insecurities and problems. I had my own to work on! I was ready to glow with the flow. I vowed to create a new movement and lead with life, my values, my dreams, my vision. And I didn't need a man to do it!

I invite you to unwrap the gift of vibrance I have carefully tied with a glorious ribbon. Find the hidden attributes you possess! Some of the items in this box wrapped with my very VIBRANT ribbon may be:

- *Laughter*
- *Humour*
- *Seeing the strengths in others*
- *Authenticity*
- *Energy*
- *Acceptance*
- *Resilience*
- *Courage*

    I hope to help others as an intentional impactor and an agent for change. I act with courage to care about myself enough to do things in the higher level of consciousness to release fear, anger, and apathy knowing these do not serve me. I activate my light not only for myself but for others. I will model what's possible. I know that if I fulfill my potential, I can show others how to do so. I want you to believe in you and that you can purposefully bring on a VIBRANT life no matter your age or circumstances, to be truly "entangled no more!"

> *We are stars wrapped in skin.*
> *The light you are seeking has always been within*
> -Rumi

    Hop aboard the VIVA space shuttle! I am excited about hosting you via my past and recent journeys to explore the 7 different stars in the VIBRANT Universe. Ready to blast off?

THE VIVA SPACE JOURNEY THROUGH HER JOURNALS

*She took a journey in outer space
Far from her present world
In a universe of past horizons
Where her history was soon unfurled.
The coloured paths that she did follow
In her shuttle blasting above
Were filled with words on pages varied
And bound in skies of love.*

*To a faraway Galaxy, a name yet unknown
Her mission was purposeful there,
To find the truth that was hidden within
And find what the gems were to share.
With much exploration she soon did discover
Seven stars meant to linger together.
Seven stars shining bright with their radiance warm
Yet each star had its own magic letter.*

*Each carried its own unique message.
Each star with its personal dream.
Each star with its traits to inherit.
Each one its own sparkle and gleam.
As she flew past the one to the other
Starting first with Star V, then Star I
Past Star B and Star R and Star A
To Stars N and Star T, then "Oh My!"*

*This Galaxy's name was spelled out!
The stars called it VIBRANT, no doubt!
Come aboard on the Viva Space Shuttle
To learn what it's truly about!*

Vivian Shapiro - January 2022

CHAPTER 2
⭐ One: VIVA LA Vs

Living a Vibrant Life is Being a Visionary, Finding your Vibe, Visualization, Creating your Vibration, Living Values & more

Be a VISIONARY

Even at the age of 5, I seemed to have had an extraordinarily huge VISION of what life was meant to be for me. But I did not know that at the time.

Did you play school when you were young? Me too! I loved to be the "teacher" and would convince my other friends that they should be the students. Somehow they agreed! When more than two of my friends were engaged in our "school days" play, I assigned myself to the role of "principal" when I didn't even really know what the role even meant. All I knew was that it was bigger, better and more important than being a student or teacher! As a young child I VISUALIZED myself at the top!

As a side note, I now know, with my educator experience, that, although the principal paycheck may be bigger, the MOST IMPORTANT people in a school community are those with the greatest impact on our youth: the classroom teacher and the front office staff!

The fact that I lived with a huge VISION as a child, was a bit of a dichotomy between the "reality" me and the "virtual" me. As an immigrant from Europe with Jewish parents from Germany who escaped the holocaust, living together with my "Omi" and "Opi", born in Portugal, but with German speaking parents and grandparents, I was a bit of an oddity. The first preschool I attended back in the late 1940s in Toronto was not as it is today, alive with mixed ethnicities, cultures and colours. I was cute but I was odd.

My parents worked long hours while I lived with my very critical and scary grandmother who was severely scarred by the unfortunate personal trials she lived and witnessed in Nazi Germany. She had watched firsthand the loss of family and was pressured to quickly escape her beloved home. Not knowing any of this, as a young child, I feared her.

I grew up introverted, afraid to speak my broken English and extremely insecure among others. However, on my own, the "virtual" me dreamed big! Big bold gargantuan dreams!.

We moved often to different Canadian cities following my dad's career journey. This constant change of friends, schools and communities did not help my self-image. At the same time, as an only child, thanks to books and places my parents took me, I visualized myself being a great dancer, an artist, an actor, a singer, always creatively thinking of me in all sorts of imaginative ways. All this before the impact of television or social media!

Finally at seven and a half years of age, a baby sister was presented to me, but we were worlds apart at that point. Other than loving to cuddle her, I barely remember her until I was 13 when I was often assigned babysitting duties! She has since forgiven me for waking her up to sleep with me, pretending she was the lonely one wanting to

ONE: VIVA LA Vs

crawl into my bed. Fact is, I still felt like an only child. I'm pleased to say that now as adults we are bonded sisters and good friends!

We moved a total of six times until my parents settled for a permanent home. I was thrilled! A two-storey but detached home in a great community very close to the high school I would be attending. Previous to this, I had attended six different schools from ages 4 to 12. Not a great way to accumulate long-term lifelong friends! I remember, however, despite being bullied, teased, chosen last for teams and not always being invited to the "popular" parties, I loved life. I may have been sad or confused, crying myself to sleep some nights, but I also remember smiling, dancing and laughing a lot!

I had other challenges. I was tagged with cruel names like "Four Eyes" as I sported corrective glasses already at the end of Grade 3. "Bucky Beaver" was my other "nom de plume" as a result of my very large front teeth and very conspicuous overbite. Most kids or teachers could not pronounce my strange German last name (Leinung) and remember, I absolutely hated my first name Vivian. My middle name was 'Tauba' which I thought was a Portuguese word for 'little doe'. The only thing close to that, was that my family indeed had "little dough". I wanted so badly to be Mary Catherine or Jane or Sally like most of the other girls!

Despite all of this, I loved to laugh, sing, dance, act and play and I absolutely loved school. I guess I was smart. I had that going for me! I "skipped" Grade 4 and was accelerated from Grade 3 to Grade 5. This may not have been wise, given as a late November birth baby, I was already younger than most of the students. I don't know what they were thinking in those days! Later in university that age difference caught up to me!

Did my dreams come true? That's for the other chapters. I'll keep you guessing for now.

The main fact was that being able to visualize on my own created for me a place where I was revered, admired, beautiful, respected and loved. Those visualizations were my wings to lift me to a place of validation.

Today as a much more spiritual being, I look back and thank those days of challenge I had as a young toddler and pre-teen. They say your setbacks set you up for your setups. They were, in fact, a blessing, as the many incidents led me to a world of dreams and desires that superseded any of the hurt or initial tears. My dad of course was heartbroken to see his first child so upset by others, but my mom did not coddle me.

My mom! A force of nature! She was the domineering alpha in our family. What she did for me was equally as loving as my dad but in a much different way. She did affirm that I was beautiful and smart and that I could be anything I wanted to be. She encouraged me to move on, to not dwell on negative experiences and to think other thoughts with promises that my tomorrows would bring a new day. In other words: Get over it! Shit happens. Some downs, some ups, so what…next!

I grew strong in my conviction to be someone special and later, as a teacher and principal, had huge empathy for any student going through similar situations.

I do not honestly know what it was in me that steered me to live vibrantly no matter what. I do know that, no matter what age, what circumstance, having a VISION of what things can be, instead of what they are, can definitely alter your life. Happy heart, healthy mind.

Be a VISIONARY! We are all born with a vivid sense of imagination! Just watch a child playing with cardboard boxes or plastic containers. Along with self satisfying visualizations, using your imagination along with your wisdom allows you to think beyond your own dreams, to the deeper level of envisioning a better world to make a difference for others. Find your true purpose as a visionary to enhance your life as you serve others. This will without a doubt keep you vibrant with purpose!

Find your unique VIBE

Never disregard a moment in time as fleeting, for in fact it could send off a whole series of incidents that result in marvellous memories yet to be.

It was an absolutely gorgeous day at the resort on Margarita Island, Venezuela. My new friend whom I had just met, Terry, and I were sitting at the pool early in the morning, discussing and sharing information about each other while our spouses were sleeping in. When getting deeper into our dreams and visions, he proposed a very interesting suggestion for me, which I will share shortly. My husband and I met him and his wife via a mix of coincidental events, obviously meant to introduce me to another aspect of living vibrantly. I love sharing this story!

Chance encounters meant to be…

The night before my husband and I were to leave for our holiday to Venezuela, we went to our favourite Chinese food place. Needing an extra chair for our table of friends who had joined us, I went over to this sweet looking young couple to ask if I could take one of theirs. A friendly conversation ensued and the chair was taken to join those at our table. I couldn't help but be drawn to the handsome-looking couple and glanced often at them, not knowing that a new journey was in store for me based on that brief encounter.

The next day at the airport was chaotic. The winter storm had caused delays in many airports. Travellers were everywhere, all chairs were occupied and the carpeted floors were a mass of bodies, coats, and carry-ons as frustrated passengers-to-be became more and more disgruntled, angry and impatient. It was not a pretty scene. Given this was March Break, I looked around to see if there were any fellow teachers I knew, with whom I could engage, knowing my husband was not in a speaking mood! And that's when I saw them, yet in the distance walking down towards the gates…the young couple from the restaurant the night before. What were the chances of that?

We decided to go to our gate and grab a piece of floor, and there they were again. I walked over. I just couldn't resist! As I approached, Terry waved at me, pointing a finger at me as if to say "You!" No, he did not recognize me from the restaurant the night before. He thought I was a friend of his named Linda. Elana however did remember and we laughed at the coincidence that here we were both going to Margarita Island. And that was that, or so I thought.

What would then be the chances of Terry and Elana sitting right next to us on the plane? As we engaged in further conversation, delighted that we were finally leaving though 5 hours late, we found out we were also going to the same resort! I love stories like this! There's more!

Although they were much younger than us, we became instantly connected . We agreed to meet up with each other for a late night-cap to unwind from the horribly long day. The plane finally lifted its wheels for an authentic take off and we all settled in to sleep or return to our chosen movies. And that's how the friendship began!

So here we were, Terry and I, early birds lounging by the pool chirping away. At one point, he noticed that I was scribing in my journal and asked: "What are you writing about?" adding, "You look very immersed in your book." I told him the whole gambit, including the mention of my poetry, disclosing that I feel I have a penchant for turning some of these into song lyrics. I continued that I can actually hear the music in my head when I write. I feel I have a vibe unique to me when I write. I read a few of my poems to him. Please note that other than my "fairly" interested husband, I had not shared these with anyone else.

He was the most intense listener and was impressed. "When we get back to Toronto, we will go out, the four of us, and I will introduce you to my younger brother. He is a very talented singer-songwriter who plays at a venue in the west end. I think you two should meet," he suggested. Do you see where this is going?

Meeting the brother…

We all became great friends. I adored his brother, Richard Samuels, a young, talented up-and-coming singer-songwriter. I shared my poems and song ideas with him and he too was impressed. After teaching me how to create chorus and bridge additions to my verses, we worked on a few songs and I was in my element. My vibe became alive and was unstoppable.

In 1992, Richard Samuels was about to be highlighted on a CD highlighting three new artists. This would then be sent to radio stations across Canada. You can imagine how elated I was to learn that one of the songs I co-wrote with him, "*Between Friends*", was to be featured on that CD. Two of Richards' songs were grabbed for cross-Canada radio airplay and mine was one! A few months later, the song I co-wrote was one of the songs on Richard's first new album.

Go Vibrant!

My song actually reached #18 on Billboard across Canada. I cannot tell you the thrill it was for me to be in the car or in a grocery store and hear the song we co-wrote blaring through the speakers! You can hear "Between Friends" on Spotify!

Before moving to California, Richard, whom I called my young "Billy Joel" friend, played at a famous piano bar, La Serre, in an exclusive hotel in downtown Toronto. How my body tingled when he announced the song he was about to play, recognizing me, his song lyricist, in the audience. I let my unique talent take its course and we created more songs together, one after my separation, a beautiful song of hope, entitled *"Time is Your Friend"*, adapted from the very words of consolation given to me by a teacher colleague when most needed. Thank you Jim Strachan!

Richard is extremely talented, with what I think was unfortunately bad management! He has that James Taylor quality mixed with the boy next door quality and appeal of a "Michael Bublé". He could have been the Bublé of his time and I regret that I did not have enough verve to try to become his manager. His albums still thrill me and I know he is still happy and content with his music producing and singing career happily living in the California sun. We are still very good friends, and maybe one day I will finish our attempt at *"But That Was Then"*, a true yet sad song about a mother, and her "found again" but later "gone again" son.

Find your VIBE! We are all unique. Find out what makes you tick and brand it! Market it! Be the vibe you strive to be! You may surprise yourself! Fuel your vigor, your verve and spirit or enthusiasm with passion, moxie, toughness, pizzazz, get-up-and-go and a sassy kick-ass demeanour! Go Vibrant YOU!

ONE: VIVA LA Vs

Create your VIBRATION

Finding this unique vibe in me, was now becoming a full VIBRATION of energy that I was creating to bring my ideas and energy to the world. You find your vibe first and then create a higher frequency by putting your thoughts, ideas and actions out there. I was ready to raise my vibration to the universe, attracting what I desired.

When different frequencies of energy occur…

My vibe became alive as a strong VIBRATION in February 1995, the year after my separation.

As the principal of Pleasant Public School (and it was pleasant!) I was working with my talented Canadian Artist and nephew Ian Leventhal to find a way for school children from different religious and ethnic backgrounds to create replicas of the various multicultural, multi ethnic, multi religious buildings in Jerusalem. These were slated to be used as centerpieces for a fundraising dinner for the Jerusalem Foundation whose mission was to enhance the quality of life for all residents in Israel regardless of their diversity. My brilliant nephew introduced my students to the culture and history of Israel and its various structures. They were taught the skill of Ian's unique way of papier-maché artistry and they proudly created magnificent pieces of art.

And that's when I knew I had to do more! I felt a vibration stir in me like no other. My thoughts led to the possibility of creating a vision of harmony in a unique song, a magnificent song that could be performed at the fundraising event. I imagined a song of peace and harmony connected with the art project and the vision of togetherness promised by the Jerusalem Foundation.

After getting approval from the board members, I immediately called my friend Richard excited for our next collaboration! He loved the idea. In his small studio I was in awe how he magically produced this beautiful melodic tune accented with a Middle East flavour.

He gave me a tape (does anyone remember those?) and on the ten minute journey home, I played it in the car. I composed the lyrics in my head as if someone was breathing life into me. I ran into my house and without taking my coat off, I scribbled down the words in a fury. It was the date of my dad's death 8 years previously and I truly believe he was there feeding me with the magic words that flowed fluidly onto paper from my writing pen! I brought them to Richard that evening and the song *"Sharing a Dream"* was born!

The next day we began to assemble willing and talented musicians, singers, and technicians who volunteered their time to create a compact disc of the song, along with two other songs by Richard. Each of the over 1000 event participants received a copy of this as a thank you for their support.

My vision did not end there. I proposed to the organizers and my nephew, a board member, that now they needed a live performance and nothing says impactful more than having young kids sing! I convinced my musical friend and principal colleague Bruce Howell, who was also part of the creation of the disc, to take time out of his own school to teach the four part harmony of "Sharing a Dream" to a select group of students from my school. I wasn't asking much!

On May 26, 1995 exactly a year after I made the decision to leave my marriage, I was being honoured, along with Richard Samuels, at The Jerusalem Foundation Fundraising Dinner with former Jerusalem Mayor Teddy Kolleck and a plethora of who's who in Toronto. The evening itself was classy, magical and inspiring. The highlight of the evening was the performance of our choir of beautiful young voices, students aged 7 to 11, who were joined by the famous Canadian Amadeus choir for the finale chorus. So emotional. There was not a dry eye in the house!

Create your VIBRATION! The frequency and energy with which you resonate will improve your life and relationships. Find mindfulness methods to help you live and show up in a high vibration frequency. When you bring your high energy and frequency to the plate, your vibrancy will create magic. When you radiate energy, you affect your life and others lives.

SHARING A DREAM
R. Samuels/V. Shapiro 1995

we have a dream, a vision that's clear
we have a dream so far away from fear
somewhere a place where we'll be strong
where we can all be belong

come with us…now let's take a chance
come to a place where we can dance
the dance of our souls they'll meet as one under the rising sun

(*Chorus) and we're sharing a dream making it seem that it can be peace and harmony
and we're sharing a dream wherever you may be
just hold out your hand for peace throughout the land

no tears to shed or sorrows we know
only a land where love will grow
tensions will die and wars will cease
dream of a land of peace

Go Vibrant!

we'll celebrate a new way to live
staging a play with words that give
hope for the world where we can find
comfort and peace of mind *

come let the music wash away the tears
the cleansing of our minds to think of future years
so we can make a land that is free, together in harmony

(5 year old student) I have a dream a vision that's clear
I have a dream so far away from fear
somewhere a place where we can find
comfort and peace of mind

la la la la la la la la la la la la la la la la la la
share in our song sing through the night
rekindle a special light

and we're sharing a dream making it seem that it can be peace and harmony
and we're sharing a dream wherever you may be
just hold out your hand for peace throughout the land.

Know your VALUES, Live your VALUES, Add VALUE to others

I have no detailed anecdote for this suggestion. It is beyond a doubt the most important V word in here. I can tell you that I try intentionally to use my values as flashlights to lighten up my doubts and as compasses that will guide my growth as a good person. The values you assign yourself are guidelines for how you behave emotionally, intellectually, in business and socially and usually form your expectations for others you keep in your circle. Along with this, live vibrantly by adding value to those in your heart, community and world! VALUE time with friends, family, with community and most of all, with and for you.

More "V"s for Vibrancy

You may have heard of Clubhouse, the app, started about the time of COVID. It is a type of social network based on voice where people around the world get together to talk, listen and learn from each other in real time. I recently co-hosted a room every Thursday/Friday evening called *"Everything is Right About Living a VIBRANT Life."* What a beautiful hour and a half spent with like-minded individuals as we discussed the positive aspects of living a joyful, purposeful life, especially when the fears of COVID were rampant. We engaged in a lively discussion which also brought forth poetry, music and indigenous flute tunes! Thank you to the participants during our V day for adding these thoughts for this chapter.

"Everything is Right About Living a VIBRANT Life" when you:

- *Celebrate your VICTORIES*
- *Practice VISUALIZATION*
- *Live with VERVE*
- *Find your VIVACIOUS overcoat*
- *Be VALIANT*
- *Breathe in VITALITY in all you do*
- *Allow and address VULNERABILITY*
- *Be an actiVIST for Social Change (poetic license for my friend Vivek)*

Go Vibrant!

Now I know you are excited to travel to the next star in GALAXY VIBRANT, but first a few more moments for you in V.

HEY VIBRANT YOU! IT'S YOUR TURN.
Take it From Here!

LIVE YOUR VISION!

Find a spot to sit or lie comfortably. Visualize yourself five years from now. Let your dreams of who you wish to be, of what you wish to achieve, of how your life will be improved, of how you will make an impact on others or your world, play into the mix of this visualization. Work it in. Massage it in. Breathe it in until you feel and sense those visions coming alive! Now answer these questions:

What does your life look like? Feel like?

_____
_____
_____
_____
_____
_____

What do your relationships with your family members look like?

_____
_____
_____
_____
_____
_____

What do your relationships with your close friends look like?

What are you experiencing that is joyful?

What kind of a life are your children experiencing? (if you have children)

Go Vibrant!

What are your biggest accomplishments?

_____
_____
_____
_____
_____
_____

What hurdles or challenges have you overcome?

_____
_____
_____
_____
_____
_____

What are you doing to serve others?

_____
_____
_____
_____
_____
_____

What are you doing to serve and take care of yourself?

_____
_____
_____
_____
_____
_____

Keep the vision alive!
Keep this somewhere you can look at often.
Revisit.
Live the vision!

THE V AFFIRMATIONS PAGE

Repeat those that you wish to apply to you today. Do so out loud!

I allow myself to VISUALIZE what is possible.

I am a VISIONARY who pictures my dreams in my future.

I have a passion to fulfill my VISION.

I live with VERVE and VITALITY.

I have a VIBE unique to me.

I create a VIBRATION in my space and in others that is alive and comfortable.

I celebrate my VICTORIES.

I am VIVACIOUS and fun.

I live with a set of VALUES I hold true and respect.

I VALUE my special times with me, my family, friends and the community.

I am VALIANT, showing courage and determination.

I allow myself to be VULNERABLE, accepting the emotional risk
that comes from being open.

CHAPTER 3
⭐ Two: INVITING THE Is

Living a Vibrant Life is living with: "I" am, Imagination, Interests, Intention, Integrity while being Interested, Interesting, Inspired, Inspiring

Invite your "I AM"!

Most importantly, being vibrant can only occur when you look after the "I" in your life… as in me myself and I! Let's discover the most important aspect of vibrancy…YOU! The "I" you bring to this world, the intimate "I", the unique, wonderful "I" that defines the special awesome you!

Some may call me over-extended, but I honestly believe that keeping busy keeps you living with vitality so that you can put your best foot forward as a vibrant, exciting person who can't wait to start each day, who looks forward to getting up and having an impact and influence on the world.

" *'I AM' are the 2 most powerful words you can use to start a sentence"*
  - Dr. Wayne W. Dyer

Shout this out loud so that the clouds can hear you say this:
"I am vibrant in all I do!"

Go Vibrant!

Now add 3 more statements that affirm that vibrancy in you

_____

_____

_____

_____

_____

SHOWING UP IN THE NOW

(on thinking about the approaching November 20 2021)

My 75th year will soon pass me by
As my 76th is now drawing nigh.
Been quite the year with stress and strife
Surviving through fears in this Covid life.
Am I getting old? Hey wait! NOT ME!
I still think and act like at least 33!
As I watch Autumn leaves that gently fall,
I think of transitions that happen to all.
Through my personal changes, I've shown up big,
Discarding those leaves that no longer give
My life its true purpose. I reveal the now!
Uncovering each day my why, what and how.
I have much to give, more to love, this I know.
Spread my power and magic with more room to grow.
Today I choose "moi" and accept what will be
Everything, yes everything is RIGHT about ME!

Vivian Shapiro - July 2021

HEY VIBRANT YOU! IT'S YOUR TURN.
Your Inner Poet

What? Already you ask? Yup! We are going to indulge in writing a poem right from the start of our journey on Star Two.

Have you ever written poetry? If not, you are about to become your own poet laureate claiming the INCREDIBLE "I" in you! It will be easy. Just follow my template while you take a trip down memory lane. They say the best copycats win so here is your chance to duplicate a poem process and make it personally yours. Here we go…

The Poem Process

The Title: I AM FROM…

(*This idea is inspired from George Ella Lyon's "Where I am From" poem, introduced to me by my wonderful No Mud No Yoga session teacher, Karen Cryer*)

For those of you having a panic attack right now, please know that this is written in free verse with no rhyming necessary! Take a breath. The words you will choose will be a way to reflect personally on your upbringing, childhood, memories and feelings via the use of your senses. Dig deep to find your ideas and words from your early childhood experiences.

The poem will consist of five stanzas
1. I am from the SOUNDS of
2. I am from the TASTE of
3. I am from the SIGHT of
4. I am from the TOUCH of
5. I am from the SMELL of

Go Vibrant!

At the end, you add a closing few lines to sum up your thoughts. Voila!

Following is the poem I wrote to give you an idea of how shallow or deep, funny or serious you may wish to get. Enjoy getting to know me better!

I AM FROM - Vivian Shapiro

I am from...The very early SOUNDS of:
Gentle waves crashing over happy children's voices
Playing in the sand on the beaches of Portugal
The later sounds of busy traffic
From the open windows of our high rise apartment in Toronto Ontario Canada
Roller skating wheels in the arena where I took lessons
And the melodious music of the 40s, coming from our old huge radio
Or played on a record player
And it surprises me that I still know the words today

I am from… The TASTE of :
My mom's German cooking
Especially the Wiener Schnitzel and apricot and brown sugar dumplings
The freshly toasted tuna fish sandwiches awaiting me for lunch
Which I ate while watching Search for Tomorrow before I had to get back to school
Coffee Crisp treats bought for me by my Opi who walked me to the variety store
Freshly popped buttered popcorn as we ate in our car at the drive-in movies

I am from The SIGHT of:
Rivers, birds, shades of green, varieties of plants, trees, well trodden paths
Of the ravines, (my temporary backyard)
Where we played in empty refrigerator boxes
Making them our imaginary homes.
Giggling friends running desperately uphill to make it back to the apartment
To avoid the sight of an upset mother who had dinner on the table.
Party sounds in our basement & Mom and Dad dancing

TWO: INVITING THE IS

I am from The TOUCH of:

My first Labrador, Nero, who slept with me

Travelled abroad with us and had to sleep in the car not allowed in our new apartment

7 years of waiting… the touch of a baby sister

Her soft dimply skin

Her fingers that curled around my thumb

The velvet costume for my ballet debut

My Opi's big tummy as he embraced me

My dad's soft lips on my forehead kissing me goodnight

I am from The SMELL of:

The ocean

Sardines on Portuguese street BBQs

My grandmother's perfume…ew!

Omi and Opi's old oak dining room furniture

Their damp basement

The lilacs in our first backyard of our first house

My dad's awful pipe smoke though I tried to avoid it, happy he finally gave it up

Every Monday, the smell of the freshly washed sheets,

That dried with the wind, outside on the line

Now on my newly made bed

I am from immigrants, Holocaust survivors, struggles, second hand clothes, strength, courage, but most of all support, love and dreams of leading my best life.

Are you ready? It's your turn…
I'd love for you to send me your poems!
Maybe we can create an ebook!
Send to vivianshapiro@rogers.com with the subject heading,
I AM FROM

Go Vibrant!

I AM FROM   by _____

I am from the SOUNDS of..

_____
_____
_____
_____

I am from the TASTE of

_____
_____
_____
_____

I am from the SIGHT of

_____
_____
_____
_____

I am from the TOUCH of

_____
_____
_____
_____

I am from the SMELL of

_____
_____
_____
_____

I am from (closing lines to sum up)

_____
_____
_____
_____

*There! Now look how interesting your life actually was
to make you who you are today!
Find a lovely piece of paper to rewrite this or file it electronically.
Be sure to place this in a spot where someone you love can find it!*

"Life whispers to you every single day from the time you wake up."
- Oprah Winfrey

IMAGINE!

If you are not already writing in a journal or scribing some of your thoughts, feelings, puzzles and adventures, I highly recommend it. Now that I have been spending more time delving into my journals, I thank my past and present self for these treasures that give me back my own memorable moments to relive my adventures and to continue to find lessons from which to learn. I sure did have a lot of imagination in those days. And still do! Never stop imagining!

The Golden Goldie Imaginative Trip…

September 2008, I came home at 3:00 in the morning from an absolutely magnificent evening of living one of my dreams. Everything I had imagined years ago actually came true, like a fairy tale. I grabbed my journal and wrote until 5:00 that morning, capturing the magical night as authentically as possible before it escaped my mind. It is for that very reason that the story I now retell, I know was not a figment of my imagination! The truth lay in the words that poured out of my hand as if it were literally a downpour. I share here some background info, and then some of the excerpts from my special evening, straight out of my journal pages written almost 14 years ago.

The birth of my imagination…

Between 1967 and 1973 I was addicted to the highly irreverent hour-long comedy variety show, *Laugh-In*. It was there that I fell in love with Goldie Hawn, my twin, my kindred spirit, my idol, my laugh buddy, and back then I vowed to meet her one day! When I found out that I was one day older than her, I knew she was my twin by another mother! When I read her book, "A Lotus Grows in the Mud", I was convinced that we were kindred spirits and I knew that it was only a matter of time and patience until we would meet.

This weekly show *Laugh-In* was a hilarious exploration of hot-button topics of the day winning many awards. Hosted by the chain-smoking straight man Dan Rowan (puffing away on the air, yes) and wiseacre Dick Martin, the show featured a talented cast of very funny actors, my favourites being Artie Johnson, Ruth Buzzi, Lily Tomlin, and Goldie Hawn, whose giggle, similar to mine, was infectious. The short skits, slapstick, running gags, traditional jokes, wacky sound effects, one-liners, dialogue bubbles, scrolling text, and

TWO: INVITING THE Is

musical numbers took your mind away from work, family and challenges for an hour of laughter. Check it out on YouTube to watch the *Laugh-In* favourites but please know that there may be some offensive material. WARNING!

I started teaching in 1968, almost 23 years old and for some reason, many of my students decided to compare me to the adorable Goldie Hawn. I was certainly flattered but at the time I did not understand it as I was brunette (then) and I can only assume it was my fun personality and the laugh. Yes definitely the laugh. Or might I say "giggle". The full turnout I experienced on curriculum night was not because the parents were all that interested in knowing about the curriculum, but more because all the parents wanted to see this "Goldie Hawn" teacher! I hope they weren't disappointed.

For years and even more so after I turned blond, many people would say to me "Do you know who you remind me of?" Although I anticipated their answer, I always asked "Who?" 98 percent of the responses: Goldie Hawn! Given her portrayal as a bit of a space cadet, dumb blond sort of character, though flattered, I used to question if that was the resemblance. And in fact that could very well have been the reason! As smart as I may have been, I did have a splash of silly.

I followed Goldie's career, watched every movie and was especially a huge fan of her Goldie Hawn Foundation "MindUP for Life" program for children. I even played Goldie Hawn characters in Cabaret shows and my own creation of The Thursday Night Live show for fellow principals.

GO VIBRANT!

Scene: Staff room

BRUCE: Vivian, are you **ambivalent** about the new curriculum?

ME: uh …um …uh …mmm. *(wide eyed)* uh, yes and no!

(big giggle)

Audience laughter

I just had to meet her! When my son Todd got into the radio business and became a pseudo-celebrity here in Toronto, very well connected with a large fan network, I told him in no uncertain terms that I was holding him responsible for getting me in the same room as Goldie Hawn before I left this world!

Fast Forward to September 2008. Below are excerpts right out of my Journal (those indented):

The Actual Golden Goldie Event 2008

My son calls me tonight and humbly apologizes for not having called or spoken to me in the last 10 days even though I have been leaving messages. He informs me that he will make it up to me big time! I have heard that one too many times. The conversation follows:

TODD: Mom, what is something you've ALWAYS wanted?

ME: *(answers hopefully but at the same time, knowing this will not be the answer)*

For you to get married!

TODD: *Laughing*

No, I am not engaged!

Two: Inviting the Is

Think more selfishly… for you!

ME: For me to still be alive by the time you get married!

TODD: (*frustrated and impatient*)

> Mom! Come on! Think of you! Think selfish! Who have you always wanted to meet??
>
> *I suddenly know what he might mean! I have to catch my breath*

TODD: (*continuing*) And what are you doing this Friday night?

ME: (*thinking*) Well, if it's who I am thinking it may be, even if I was meeting with George Clooney, I'd cancel it!

TODD: Well mom, you are going to meet GOLDIE HAWN!

ME: Really OMG OMG how? what ? when? where???

TODD: Settle down mom. Find something really nice to wear.

> I'm taking you to the Sick Kids Car Rally Fundraiser. Goldie Hawn is the chair and hopefully we will meet her in the VIP section …no promises but let's see what we can do. I have been invited as a celebrity guest and I am taking you!

ME: (*from my closet looking at what outfit I could wear*)

> THANKS. I LOVE YOU!!! OMG! mmmm…What would Goldie wear?
>
> I couldn't believe it! I was going to meet Goldie Hawn!!

Have INTERESTS, Be INTERESTED, Be INTERESTING

Preparing myself for the venue, I promised myself to be INTERESTED first, INTERESTING next and then share my

Go Vibrant!

personal INTERESTS! I read her book again, more articles on her foundation and mindfulness mission, and was surprised to see that I already had created a list of questions to ask her if I ever did meet her. I was prepped and ready!

Friday night arrived. My 64-year-old self got all dolled up in my new Louis Cerrano cocktail dress, made to look a bit funky over skinny ankle leggings, strapless gold-heeled and black shoes, sporting a Goldie Hawn type hairdo by Giancarlo, my hair stylist for the past 35+ years. Truth is I always wear my hair like that! I was ready to rock and roll.

> Before we depart, I get the lowdown on what I should and shouldn't do at the venue. Apparently there will be many celebrities there. Apparently Todd will not approach them; he waits for them to approach him. I am anxious to see how this will all play out. We have some wine together…he has loosened himself up, and I am ready to ROAR!
>
> We taxi (Uber did not exist at that time) to the venue (plug for MUSIK) and get the red carpet treatment, hosted by stunning sexy tall Nicole, who seems to know Todd well. What stunning sexy tall woman in this city doesn't know Todd?
>
> The place is hopping! The free bar station welcomes me with one of the many Cosmo Martinis of the night. As we passed by on the red carpet, cameras flashing, I noticed Goldie being interviewed by Etalk. She was wearing a similar black cocktail dress to mine but with a blazer over it! She is so me! I usually wear a blazer over things! Why didn't I? I cursed!

TWO: INVITING THE IS

Up close and personal with Goldie...

Todd and I hung out, drank, ate, and socialised with the many Canadian celebs there and sure enough, they approached Todd first, mostly with "Hey man", or "Hey brother what's up?" And they learned and seemed impressed that I was his mother!

Goldie by now was eating in a small area a few steps up from the masses known as the VIP section which could hold at best maybe 25 people. She seemed to be with a personal assistant, clipboard in hand, obviously ready to serve her instructions for Goldie's next move.

After a while, the owner of MUSIK, Stavropol, hosted us up the steps to the VIP section just as Goldie was being ushered down by a gentleman and her PA, clipboard still in hand. I said something truly stupid like: "OH! Hi! I'm going up and you are going down!" Like seriously? Did I really say that? Great move Vivian! I prayed she had not heard me.

Her welcoming speech over, Goldie proceeded back to the VIP section, led by her PA but did not go up the steps. She stayed below talking to organizers. Todd tells me, "Mom this is your only chance," and grabs my hand. (I guess this high level star is one you do approach!)

He moves over to her and says "Hi Goldie...before you leave, how about a quick photo of you and my mom who coincidentally share the exact (just a one day little white lie) same birthday as you", to which she replies in a most friendly manner with that famous smile of hers! "Sure!" I said something which I totally forgot now, but it must have been funny because she laughed.

Unfortunately the camera (yup…not a cell phone!) was on the wrong setting and the 3 photos came out fuzzy. Darn!

As she was about to part, I looked her straight in the eye, and asked her if she was coming back to the VIP section, as I would have loved to engage with her about her Mind Up program she created. She looked at her PA who seemed to nod a NO, but Goldie looked at me and said: "Um yes…or at least I'll try!"

Time out to restore the exploding heart beat: as if I had just climbed Mount Kilimanjaro!

I stayed in the area, munching, drinking, meeting sponsors, VIPs, taking photos, and watching the sexy women flaunting themselves all over Todd. I resign myself to the fact that she is not returning, and am grateful for the 10 second greeting. However, after much socializing, I notice Goldie and her PA suddenly standing alone in the corner of the VIP room, gazing over the railing into the crowd below. I knew she came back for me. I just knew it! Why else would she be back? I grabbed my camera to hang on my wrist and braved the walk towards a woman with whom I have been enamoured and by whom I have been inspired for years. It was not all about her Hollywood Star Status! Not at all.

After approaching her confidently, with bright eyes and a grateful smile, I thanked her for returning and immediately engaged her in a very long discussion of her mindfulness programs and my interest in bringing this to the Toronto District School Board. She was thrilled to participate in and answer questions. She asked me what I did and listened as I told her about my teaching, administrative career and present role as education director working with disenfranchised youth. Her

TWO: INVITING THE IS

entire demeanor changed from "celebrity" to "friend' giving me her whole attention.

At one point during our lively, vivacious conversation, she grabbed my arm and divulged with her famous Goldie Hawn smile, "My goodness, I feel like I'm talking to me!" at which point I opened the floodgates. I proceeded to tell her about my history of being told that I remind people of her. I also told her how my husband was her biggest fan and because he couldn't have her, he took me, calling me "his Goldie". She giggled and asked "And what was wrong with me?" to which I responded, "Hmmm… something about a guy named Kurt!" We laughed and giggled and talked like girlfriends. It was surreal!

I looked over at Todd who gave me a thumbs up, and told me later we looked very cute together and he was truly amazed how much time Goldie was spending with me. As well, he thought, "Oh good! One more step closer to Kate Hudson!"

I made her laugh again and she remarked "You're adorable!" I replied "No! You're adorable!" We turned to her PA and giggled and sang in unison "We are adorable!" My sides ached from laughter. Goldie added to her assistant "She could be my sister". I added, "But one day older!" (whoops the truth was out!)

We were having such a good time and she was genuinely intrigued with my life. We discussed how I could be of help to her mission and bring her program to Toronto and exchanged cards! Hers listed her foundation E.D. She saw my camera and asked her PA to take a photo requesting that I send it to her. This photo, so much better than the fuzzy ones taken earlier on the steps, showed two friends together, not a celebrity with a

73

fan! She then left the room, waved and said "Goodbye sis from another mother!"

My heart be still!

Feeling empowered by our connection, and looking forward to following up with the administrator of her organization for more work with the foundation, I walked back to Todd who greeted me with "WOW! Good for you mom!" It's not often I can impress my son.

We left later to hang around where Lindsay Lohan was doing her gig, but I could care less. I was still dizzy with the ecstasy I felt over my encounter with Goldie!

You might be wondering why I shared this story with you. I believe the magic of that moment happened because of who I am as a person who is INTERESTED in others, INTERESTING as a person and has many INTERESTS that I love to share passionately and vibrantly with those who will listen. This creates a frequency that attracts like-minded people.

We personally did not work together. I did, though, use her organization and her work to enhance my own work with youth.

Two: INVITING THE IS

Be the Sculptor for Your IMAGINATION

Michelangelo, perhaps history's greatest sculptor, understood this concept to his bones. Two of his more famous quotes speak directly to it:

"Every block of stone has a statue inside it
and it is the task of the sculptor to discover it."
"I saw the angel in the marble and carved … until I set him free."

IMAGINE YOUR PIECE OF MARBLE

Live your life as an artist.
Think like Michelangelo.
Your life is like a hunk of stone.
Imagine all the ideas and intentions you have for this stone
that can set it free from its common form.
Carve it with vivid dreams,
Chisel in your aspirations,
Smooth it in places with your spiritual thoughts,
Detail it with aspirations.
They all reside inside that hunk of stone
Already placed
whether by a divine light
or your vibes set out by your imagination.
Let your own vibrant actions be the tools
in which your own imagined art of self can be revealed
and brought forth into the world
for you
and others
to enjoy!!

Vivian Shapiro - May 2021

Set INTENTIONS

Setting intentions that I purposefully set forth during my meditations and yoga practices drives me to create opportunities for myself that are exciting and come to fruition. I visualized myself speaking to Goldie Hawn years before. My IMAGINATION of that moment was made real by the INTENTIONS I set forth. Each time it appeared as a very friendly conversation between two people who shared many common values and passions. When it finally occurred, it became that reality just as I had envisioned. Your imagination and intentions can create wonders! What you think about, you can bring about!

Be INSPIRED !

Be INSPIRED by others and Be INSPIRING

Your energized electricity can light up even the dark spaces you enter and empower others with your light that charges up new possibilities! Your energy is your greatest currency.

Who inspires you? Who will you inspire?

Dr. Joe the joke doctor…

My "inspirational influencers" list has many names of the people I was so fortunate to have come into my life to instill within me their magic vibrancy. I was blessed with many role models. I found many notes and passages in my journals dedicated to lessons I was learning from others. Many of these people did not even know how highly I regarded them. Or that they were my mentors!

One such name is a must to be included in here. I met Dr. Joe Leventhal when I was 19 years old, about to be engaged to my first husband, who was Dr. Joe's brother-in-law. Joey, as I called him, was 45 when I met him. Yesterday, July 2022, I had a visit with him in his own apartment at the ripe old age of 102! Interestingly I was starting this chapter and so Joey was very much on my mind!

In the 28 years I was married, Joey was the man "I wanted to be when I grew up". I looked up to him with deep affection. I did not have to look too far up, for Jo Jo, as his grandkids named him, was and is even more so today, short in height, though gigantically tall in character! One of my regrets of divorcing my then husband was that I would not have as much contact with his side of the family, particularly this one-in-a-million brother-in-law. Along with feisty Rita, his wife (my then husband's sister), the two of them were a dynamic duo of strength, a couple truly in love, with such mutual adoration and respect for each other. He was a role model for everyone and together they personified true love, forever cherished. Though Rita passed several years ago, Joey is still devoted to her memory and very much still in love.

At one hundred and two years of age, Joey had not lost his amazing sense of humour, his quick wit, his gift of the vernacular, and to my delight, his memory of the times I was in his life. He entertained me for two hours with jokes, his poems, compiled in an anthology by his granddaughter, stories of the past, tales of his offspring and he presented me with a painting he had created for me the morning before! At 102 years of age! Amazing! I will forever be inspired by Joe!

Here is the limerick I wrote for Joey for his 100th birthday:

LIMERICKS TO JOEY ON THE OUTSTANDING OCCASION OF HIS 100TH

There is a fine gent name of Joe
Boasting bagfuls of jokes he does know.
Now 100 his age
And he's still all the rage
Many anecdotes ready to go!

This doctor named Joe is no bore.
Treated patients well past eighty-four!
Was a pilot…no jest!
And an artist…the best!
Dr. Joe you're my hero for sure!
Vivian xox

Vivian Shapiro - July 2020

And as coincidences do happen to me, in searching for a photo of Joe, when I came home, I found this very old note written to me on a sheet from his 'Dr. Joseph I. Leventhal's prescription pad'. This was over 30 years old, written in blue pencil-crayon and was most likely originally taped on the back of one of his paintings he gave me as a gift.

To Viv
On your birthday,
a tribute to your Vibrancy
Verve and Vivacity.
We are all shaped and fashioned by those we love.
Joe

TWO: INVITING THE IS

The V.s were all capitalized and drawn in heavier lead. Do you think he knew then, that many years later I would write a book about that very essence of my being?

Another inspiration walks into my life…

This handsome gentleman was escorted by my secretary into my vice principal's office, just newly inhabited by me in my first year of promotion. The principal, Marion Joyce, one of my greatest mentors of all time, delegated tasks to me when she became too busy.

When the refined Herb Carnegie walked into the school as a cold call to see the principal, Marion must have signaled to our wonderful secretary to send him to me. It was my lucky day! My life was about to change, as was my future life that I was not even yet contemplating.

Herbert H. Carnegie sat on my couch graciously thanking me, in that soft but confident tone, and proceeded to tell me his purpose for visiting our school. I let him talk and was mesmerized by his story, his vision and his request and we bonded immediately.

I invite you to google Herb Carnegie and read about his full story. In short, Herb is often called "the best player who never played in the NHL". As a child Herb spent hours on the frozen ponds near his home, and when they couldn't get a puck they used frozen horse turds. He made history when he played in a semi-professional league in the late 1940s on an all-black line. But he never made it to the NHL, which was his ultimate dream. Despite the fact that he was an MVP three times, they brought up other players of lesser caliber. Yes, racism was a large factor! In fact, Herb at 18 heard the Maple Leafs owner, scouting at the time, say "I'd take him tomorrow if…I would give anyone $10,000 if they could turn Carnegie's skin white." Can you imagine how he felt? Even in his late 80's he would cry about it.

Herb was so devastated that he vowed to change the course for young people coming into an unfair world. Later when he turned to making a living in the insurance business, he wrote a creed of living called The Future Aces Creed. He started the first hockey school in Canada, where he promoted good citizenship, teaching the game of life along with hockey skills, and founded the Herbert H. Carnegie Future Aces Foundation.

And why was he here sitting with me in my office? He and his wife Audrey and sometimes his daughter Bernice, were making appearances in schools to pass on the Future Aces message and give all students a Future Aces creed (www.futureaces.org) He showed me a copy of the creed. My heart melted. I was intrigued. I immediately saw the need for and value of introducing our entire school community, staff, parents, and students to this man and his creed. I did not hesitate.

Together Herb and I made a plan for him and his wife to come to a staff meeting to present their story and to explain the creed. The idea would then be to get feedback from a survey I would draw up about how each staff member felt about various aspects of bringing this philosophy to the school, engaging the students in learning how to be a Future Ace and using the creed for announcements, awards etc. I brought him with me across to the next office, to meet the principal and discuss our proposal. I adored this woman, Marion Joyce, my mentor. She had great trust in my skills to lead. Two years prior when she was chosen to head up this new open concept K to 8 school, she hired me as a teacher and witnessed how I filled various leadership positions in the school. She chose me to fill in the role of VP when it was vacated two years later.

She smiled her gracious smile, shook Mr. Carnegie's hand and said to him, "I am delighted to have you on board," and it was then we set the staff meeting up. Marion gave me carte blanche with this as my project and I ran with it…in fact I flew with it!

Herb changed my life. He changed the way I looked at staff and children. He changed the way I looked at problems, how I became a forward thinker, a problem solver, a student mediator and the list goes on. He softened my approach to life and my old-fashioned ideas of discipline to be more understanding of the other person's perspective (although my own young children would probably not agree with that!) He was magic! I adored him! He was my angel and my inspiration.

In the years that followed, with other supporting principals, I created many ideas, bringing the Future Aces creed off the poster of the walls of a school into a living breathing mechanism that permeated the very raison d'être of our school community! In the next 3 schools in which I was a principal, Future Aces became alive and blossomed and Herb was an important fixture, for assemblies, classroom visits, and awards nights, even when he began to lose his sight due to glaucoma! He didn't miss a beat.

I became a board member of The Herbert H. Carnegie Future Aces Foundation. Later, immediately upon retirement from The Toronto District School Board, at the age of 54, I was asked to become the first Education Director for the foundation, to spearhead even more wonderful projects in a plethora of school communities where we could make a difference. Now I was able to inspire others as Herb had done for me!

Go Vibrant!

Maturing with Carnegie…

My best moments were as Herb's driver (after his blindness set in) so that I could get him to our many keynote presentations. Herb with his white stick, me with the rap I made up for the kids! We were quite the team. Our drives to the school and back created more magical moments for us as we talked about everything under the sun and I was privy to so many stories he had about his youth. We even sang songs together! And we laughed a lot! He had an infectious laugh. In fact I am good friends with his youngest daughter Rochelle and she has that same laugh!

Until his departure from this world at 91, Herb and I remained good friends. One memory we had that we truly deemed as an LOL moment was this one. I would hold Herb's arm tightly as we walked into the school and we had a rhythm that allowed him to feel safe without his cane leading him. Until that one day. It was the middle of winter and I had not realized how slippery the walk was. I lost my balance and when trying to retrieve it, Herb, realizing he might be in danger, dropped his cane and put his two hands forward to protect himself from any fall he envisioned having. Accidentally his hands cupped my chest, under a coat mind you, but they were there nonetheless! Awkwardly, we both landed upright and the fear of falling was no longer a concern.

>ME: Oh Herb. I am so so very sorry
>
>HERB: *(with a big grin)* The pleasure was all mine!
>
>>We laughed so hard we almost both peed in our pants!

As I write this chapter of my book, on July 10 2022, I am delirious with joy to hear the long-awaited decision to induct Dr. Herbert

H. Carnegie posthumously into the NHL Hockey Hall of Fame in the Builder category. Congratulations to the family for what should have been an honour bestowed many years ago. I can see Herb smiling his big grin from above!

I hope you have inspirers in your life. Look back and see who your influencers were and are and I am not talking about social media stars! I mean the ones who have helped you grow personally.

INSPIRE others

Music to my Ears…

While working with Future Aces, I also volunteered as the artistic director for a group known as "TDSB Cabaret Singers" (mentioned before). It used to be a North York School Board Music initiative, run by board music department staff which they could no longer fund. To keep it going, a group of us diehards decided to do everything we could to keep it alive by assuming different roles as our own Production company. In order to hire a professional musical director, we would charge fees for anyone wishing to join. 96 per cent of our cast rejoined! And there I was leading with a group of music lovers who believed the show must go on!

It was there that I met sweet Amanda Fingerhut, a teacher, who had been encouraged to join the group by a colleague of hers. Little did she know that my husband, on a Sober Driving Committee with her, had already told me that she produces shows at her high school as he informed me that she was going to join the cabaret group. Little did she know, her life was about to change. Little did she know I was already eyeing her to fill in as producer of the show to help me in my role as Artistic Director. Some people just come into your life for the right reason at the right time in the right place! This was such a time!

Of course she said "yes." That was the start of an amazing friendship of left and right brain creatures that began our collaborative projects to inspire and encourage others.

Along with an extraordinary group of TDSB volunteer staff, and the talented musical directors we employed, many fun filled three-night shows were created with Amanda and me at the helm. Together we inspired others to get up on stage and strut their stuff. My box of thank you letters is filled with gratitudes of us bringing them to life, kicking their butts to do things they never would have done, renewing their image of themselves and of giving them confidence. The list goes on and on. Keeping Cabaret alive for years was darn hard work on Amanda and me but the rewards were well worth it! Along with our amazing production team we put on quite the razzle dazzle for a bunch of amateurs!

Enabling Youth…

Now if that wasn't enough, the best was yet to come. Amanda and I were just getting started! Our greatest accomplishment in life, I believe to be our flagship contribution to the community, was the coordinated conception and implementation of *FACES…Future: A Conference Empowering Students*, a life-changing 3-day 2-night conference held in Ontario resorts, designed for youth aged 12 to 15. This was later changed to *Future: A Conference Empowering Self*. Why? Because the teaching staff that attended said that it was game changing for them as well!

And how did this come to be? The magic of two people on a mission to serve others!

While I was organizing Cabaret and presenting and working Future Aces magic in many schools across the board, I decided to present to the Future Aces Board of Directors a fully detailed proposal for a three-day Future Aces conference that could change students' lives. They loved the idea. The only thing holding us back was funding. The fundraising committee said they would work on it. That never happened! Until I met Amanda.

As we worked together for long hours on Cabaret, we slowly became very close friends despite the age difference. It worked. I had a youthful mindset and Amanda…is an old soul! A strange combination of two ages thirty-one years apart which I will touch upon later!

After pouring out to Amanda my ideas for my vision of a Future Aces Conference, she excitedly interrupted me with, "That's what I do! I have run and organized youth conferences for TAID 'Take Action on Impaired Driving' but our charity is no longer running. I can show you how to create a budget, get you a resort location, get funding, speakers, and lots more! I can do this with you!" It was like she was on speed!

With just a change of content to align to the mission of the Herbert H. Carnegie Future Aces Foundation, we created a truly life-changing conference for youth and school communities that continued for 17 years until COVID curtailed the opportunity. Through the years, our fabulous team was unstoppable! (Thank you Rochelle Carnegie, Gail James, Jenn Poirier, Dianne Leggatt, Dilaila Longo, Kalyna Bobyk)

We had no idea how powerful this event would be until we received the many accolades of how many lives we changed. We had provided hope and inspiration for participating students, our university leaders and teachers alike. It feels so good to know that 200 different students and their teachers went back to their school communities each of those 17 years spreading the Future Aces word, sharing the creed and implementing a character building project for their school that later, at the one-day Returning Faces Session, would be proudly shared by each school to their fellow delegates. Talk about a big ripple effect!

Our Ace Leaders, all volunteers, many who started out as delegates from attending schools, became a bonded family and spread their inspiration to their home group of students and also with each of the peer leaders. The rewards were too many to mention and to this day keep my heart full!

I was blessed to receive The Amazing Aces in Action Award for my work with Future Aces and the distinguished Toronto Waterfront Celebrating Outstanding Women Award in 2018 for Philanthropist of the Year.

I wish I could share with you the many forms of communications I've received over the years from those I've touched or inspired even in a small way from students I taught, teachers I led, Cabaret members I encouraged, younger friends I've adopted, and those inspired by my visits to schools, and conferences in honour of Herb's legacy. I believe I was meant to inspire others.

These things keep you VIBRANT. When you realize that you are here to serve and not only be, and not only do, but give!

As I write this rough draft of my book, I stop to check into my iPhone for messages etc. An extraordinary thing has happened. A moment of synchronicity! I have just been "dinged" with a Facebook notification. I check to see that I have been tagged on a Facebook post by Marianne Patterson, whom I taught in both Grade 5 and 6 in the 1970s!…and this was the post:

"I've reconnected with friends that I worked with 28 yrs ago and even a special woman who helped shape me and always encouraged me, my grade 5 & 6 teacher Vivian Shapiro. To have your favourite teacher actually remember you after 45 years…it just reiterates what a special woman she is."

TWO: INVITING THE IS

I have had many heartwarming messages from former students, and this one, received five months ago on a text to me, was mind blowing! I proudly share this with you too!

"Hi Viv, in the last couple of years I have become certified as a coach. One project was to create a board of the women we look up to. This is mine! …You absolutely had to be in my group of lady greats!!!... Honouring you!"

Her graphic board depicted colour photos of 9 women in individual circles with an elegantly scribed title 'lady power' by Jill Farren. I was on the top left corner of a tic tac toe grid in the company of…wait for it…Diane Keaton, Lady Gaga, Oprah Winfrey, Crystal Andrus Morissette, Kelly Ripa, Michelle Obama, Jane Fonda and Jennifer Lopez! I'm still stunned and humbled!

I am grateful for the many young people, now much older, who have reached out to me to let me know how I impacted their lives. I am even grateful for those few who have called me the B word too! Thank you also, for making me look inward.

And then there are some thank-yous that really stand out, as in the case of Jake! Jake tagged me about ten years ago to let the Facebook world know I was responsible for saving his life! What? I had done what? That cute little boy I had for Grades 4 and 5? Of course I had to immediately know what it was I had done as his teacher for I honestly did not know. I insisted we meet! Jake, now standing tall, a handsome chiselled but very hairy face replacing that cute impish look he had as a ten-year-old, disclosed his story. Jake told me he was seriously bullied in school and very depressed, unbeknownst to me. He had suicidal thoughts and was ready to take his life at any moment. But he found something different that school year, someone who actually actively listened to him. Me! He acknowledged that I candidly started paying attention to him in a way no one had

GO VIBRANT!

before! I learned a lot that day about him and me. I learned that if you act with care and love to help others feel like they are unique, special and cared for, no matter what, it may make a difference for someone and you may never know! It doesn't take much.

It's all these special unexpected moments like this that make you realize the importance of inspiring others. When you inspire others to turn a corner, to defeat their challenges, you create a legacy. You live on in the hearts of those you have touched!

HEY VIBRANT YOU! IT'S YOUR TURN.
Short and Sweet

Who is or has been your inspiration? How have they inspired you? Make a list of 3 people and beside each one, tell how you have been impacted and how you have grown.

_____
_____
_____
_____
_____

Who do you inspire? Think of 3 people you have inspired to do something different in their life. How do you believe you inspire or have inspired each of them?

_____
_____
_____
_____
_____

When you inspire others, think about the legacy you leave when you no longer inhabit our world, leaving it better than when you arrived in it!

Speaking of legacy, my Arbonne team was recently on a John Maxwell Master Class led by one of my amazing coaches, Jerry Roisentul, who was giving us an acronym for the word LEGACY. The class was on Zoom (thank you COVID) and I could see everyone, head down writing madly to get his acronym written out, while listening to the added details.

As I was busy with my own note taking, I received that familiar ding on my phone of the notification of a text I had just received. Yes, I looked! Who doesn't? It was from my friend and colleague Rochelle Carnegie who was in the Zoom class. What I received made my heart sing!

I printed it and pasted it into my journal. This is what it said:

Leadership
Enthusiasm
Generosity
Authenticity
Compassion
Youthfulness

This is you in spades. Thank you for being you …a great leader!
xo Rochelle

Thank you Rochelle! You made my day.

Live with INTEGRITY

Undoubtedly, caring for yourself to preserve your unique and special "I" is of utmost importance. The vibration and energy you get from imagining, being interested in others, being interesting for others, finding your true intention for impact, and inspiring and influencing others all embody a VIBRANT you. Let us add the biggest "I" ingredient of all! INTEGRITY. To be genuinely vibrant and spread joy and kindness, you have to be genuine, trustworthy, accountable and live by a high set of standards. Integrity improves and influences your I factor. INTEGRITY is the ultimate investment you make to have a strong foundation for your VIBRANT home!

THE I AFFIRMATIONS PAGE

Repeat those that you wish to apply to you today. Say them out loud.

I am IMPORTANT and practice pouring into myself.

I IMAGINE life being the best of all possible worlds.
I am insightful, intuitive and IMAGINATIVE.
My IMAGINATION is vast, expansive and endless.
My limitless IMAGINATION excites me.

I am INTERESTED in learning about me and those around me.
I stay INTERESTING to exude vibrancy.

I live with INTENTION.

I find people who INSPIRE me to be my best self.
I follow the light to INSPIRE me.
I INSPIRE others to lead their best life.

I live with INTEGRITY living in accordance with my deepest values.

And others, thanks to my Clubhouse friends!

I use INTERNAL INSIGHTS to live a vibrant life.

I INTEGRATE my life to support love.

I am living my best INDUSTRIOUS self.

I IMPROVE to become the best version of me.

I use INTUITION to honour what my soul needs.

I ILLUMINATE the positive.

CHAPTER 4
⭐ Three: SO B IT!

Living a Vibrant Life means being Bold and Brave with Belief, Bodaciousness and Badassery

HEY VIBRANT YOU! IT'S YOUR TURN.
Be the B!

Before we start this chapter, just for fun, fill this out. Don't overthink it. Just fill out the acronym for BOLD with whatever comes to mind!

To Live My VIBRANT life means BEING BOLD by:

B _____
O _____
L _____
D _____

Here is my attempt, and I am doing this during my rough draft writing of this book and so I am having to think on the spot also! Just like you!

GO VIBRANT!

For ME, To Live My VIBRANT life means BEING BOLD by:

B   **Believing** enough in my talents, skills and abilities that I know I can try anything!
O   **Opening** up my mind to all that's possible!
L   **Listening** to what leaders do to be successful
D   **Discarding** and **Dismissing Debbie Doubt** whenever she interferes!

Be BOLD

It All Started with a boy…

The start of my BOLDNESS came with the emergence of my self esteem and confidence. That all started with a BOY liking me. As much as I hate to admit it (because for youth today I think things would be much different) I am being BOLD and outright! Please don't judge! It did start with a boy!

It didn't matter how often my mother told me I was beautiful, all I could see in the mornings as I gazed into the mirror by the door were those cats' eyes glasses and the mass of freckles on my face and entire body. To make matters worse, a small but very dark freckle was noticeable right at the tip of my nose! I basically had a freckle frenzy tantrum every morning. Those were the days when girls (well most girls) did not wear ANY makeup to school (or ever), though some did the sneaky "wax on wax off" routine before and after school in the washrooms. Not me! I knew my mom had eyes everywhere! Thus there was no such thing as coverup for these unsightly marks, especially the dark spot in the middle of my nose, the bane of my existence, so much so that even my yearbook comments give evidence to its existence.

I digress! In Grade 10 despite my insistence that I was ugly, the boy who sat behind me noticed me for something other than my thoughts. Jim flirted with me often and the teasing about the black freckle on the tip of the nose became actually quite sweet! We were "sort of" boyfriend and girlfriend that year but in a very quiet low-key way! There was no going steady or going on dates. In school and school events, we spent a lot of time together with others. For a very very handsome young man with great physical presence, he was extremely shy. The fact that he liked to hang out with me lifted my confidence in who I was and who I could be!

I became bolder! History, with one of my favourite teachers, Mrs. Gillette at Northview Collegiate Institute, was unfortunately my worst subject, achieving a low 50's at best. That was about to end. I BOLDLY proclaimed that I would get the required B average that term to join the History Club for their trip to NEW YORK CITY! Why? I had no interest in The History Club! Yech! I knew however that smart Jim was going to be on that trip! Mrs. G. just gave me this smile that was somewhat encouraging but at the same time doubting. (Or I imagined that.)

Well, did I go? Of course I did! With a B+ average that term!

As much as I loved being in NYC for only the second time in my life, the first being when I was two years old landing by boat as a little Portuguese kid, I wasn't there for the history and events and visits. I was there for (and it's a B word at that…) a BOY! I know…shoot me now! That was however the reality!

Go Vibrant!

Four things happened on that trip:

I. A boy liked me and made me feel "pretty and witty and wise", and I felt a new boldness in me to "do me" and the Freckle Frenzy tantrums disappeared.

II. I obtained a new appreciation for History and learned more in that subject area, though I never managed an A, which I managed to get in all other subject areas! Mrs. Gillette, who treasured her calling as a teacher instilling in us a love of History, was pleased at my B+ and I think I became her favourite that year!

III. The tour of the United Nations made me dream BIG (another B word) and with my strengths in languages, I declared that I was going to be an official language interpreter for the United Nations, for all the big shots! Yessir, BIG and BOLD dreams!

IV. And some silliness: I stopped wearing my glasses and walked around semi-blind most of the time because I could recognize friends by the way they walked and gained a hearing sensitivity to voices. Yes, I grew vain. Glasses were only for classes! (Those whom I failed to recognize just thought I was a snob.)

Jim and I remained good friends throughout our high school years. I think in fact from my reunion recollection, he married a lovely Northview girl, who was a favourite friend of mine!

Jim/James: If you ever end up reading this book, please know that I forgive you for drawing the dot on my nose (so carefully originally erased by the grad photographer) and for writing in my graduation yearbook: "One of these days, you'll find some guy with a spotted nose, Good hunting!"

Three: So B It!

Young love, first love…

My real authentic high school sweetheart I met the next year, same scenario, him sitting behind me in many of my classes and teasing me during class. I guess in those days, teasing was the "come on" line. I even remember, breathlessly, the dress I was wearing the day he said "I like your dress!" It was a green polkadot dress with frilly lace and puffy sleeves, scooped neck, puffy skirt, and I'm sure I looked like a Swedish girl tending to sheep, but I was well-endowed for a 15-year-old going on 16 and that may have well been the attraction. Too bad all he saw was the back most of the time! I was so naive. I had no idea what boys were attracted to!

Jeff was popular. He was the boyfriend you remembered in high school. For my 16th birthday in November 1961 he gave me 16 red roses and took me out the day after he got his driving license to a very fancy place called "The Old Mill" in Toronto. Of course he was also the first person to take me to the high school prom! He was the one who made me feel smart and talented and beautiful, especially since he broke up with whom I considered a dynamite stunning girl, to be with me. Because I was the events yearbook editor, though not voted Queen and King of that evening, I placed our photo dead centre on the adjoining prom page!

I became BOLDER and braver with a new belief in myself. Yes, I admit that this "new me" was initiated by a BOY, a young 16/17 year old boy. I started joining all sorts of clubs and leading many high-school activities. Though I always saw myself as unathletic, a dancer but not an athlete, I BOLDLY decided to try out for the high school cheerleading squad and spent all month practising all the moves. I was ready! But I did not make the team. All of last year's popular, but very sweet attractive cheerleaders (no mean girls here!) had come back to try out so it was stiff competition. Apparently though,

Go Vibrant!

I was the bridesmaid in the competition and when one of the girls became ill, they asked me to sub! Oh joy! I was in my element. What a BOLDNESS booster! Most people today who know me are not surprised I was a cheerleader!

The other thing I did was BOLDLY apply to be a waitress at a lake resort very near Jeff's cottage so that I could be near him for a few weeks. I loved this new sense of me I was becoming. It was more in line with my dreams and visions I had for myself as a young child. This is something I NEVER would have done in the years before. I was usually more comfortable staying home with my family and close friends and would not think of straying away to lands unknown to me. I learned a lot the summer of my 16th approaching 17th year!

I am not sure what caused Jeff to write me the Dear John (or Dear Jane) letter just a week before school started the following year. We were different religions but I don't think it mattered to him, maybe to his parents, but it was never explained. I think it was just a "freedom" thing. To this day I remember my girlfriend Judy and I sitting by her fireplace burning up his letter piece by piece. The songs "*Sealed with a Kiss*" by Brian Hyand and "*See You in September*" by the Happenings were my tormentors. My first real heartbreak!

I was not looking forward to my Grade 13 year. Of course Jeff and I were assigned to the same homeform room 13C, even though there were 8 other possibilities where we could have been in different classes! There he was sitting behind me in the chemistry lab homeform room! We both thought we might reunite at one point early in the year, but the fateful football game I couldn't go to turned his interest to one of the sweet cheerleaders with whom I was a friend and that was that.

Here is the good news! It wasn't all about the BOY anymore. I focussed on ME and what I needed to do to live my dreams. I could

Three: So B It!

see it now. Ta da! Chief Head of Language Interpreters for the United Nations! I focussed that year on good marks, still having fun with lots of various people, dating many great guys, joining singing groups, stage and drama productions, trips to Quebec City (yes I got another B+), Yearbook Social Editor, and Synchronized Swimming Team. I especially wanted to get great marks because I had set my sights on university.

In those days, nursing school, teachers' college (before it required a degree) and business school were the options often sought out by women. That's just the way it was! Of my graduating class of women, I believe only about ten of us, if that, went on to university. I did not receive the Ontario Scholarship Award requiring 80% but I came darn close and was accepted by University of Toronto, University College, for which I ended up becoming HEAD CHEERLEADER for 3 years! You just have to wait for some things to come to you!

What happened to Jeff?

I know some of you are wondering. As if our lives were meant to be intertwined in our futures, we kept running into each other: when he was in Medicine at U of T, commencement, the high school reunion, etc. Each time it was a great experience. It was obvious we were still fond of each other and cared for each other, in a "friend" way. We even bumped into each other in a movie lineup as couples when we were both just married and we were both so happy for each other.

Many years later, when I was an acting principal back in 1984, I needed to use a telephone book to look up a venue for the Grade 6 graduation. (Anyone reading this remember what a telephone book is?) The top of these books gave you guides of the first and last surnames to be found on that page and in this case it was his surname, recognizable because of its unusual spelling. Sure enough at the end of the column was his name with a Dr. in front of it and with an office number as well.

I looked at the date on my calendar. Something made me look. Can you believe it was the date of his birthday! (I only remembered this because it's a famous day of the year and hard to forget.) Too coincidental to let this go, I called the number and wished him a Happy Birthday on the "answering machine", confident that the voice on the message was indeed his. Forgetting that he would not be familiar with my married name, I mistakenly concluded by saying, "This message has been brought to you by a person from your past, Vivian *Shapiro*", and left my school number. Turns out his sister-in-law has the same first and last name as me and it was all very confusing for him. We did actually connect and he finally figured out who I was! We set a time to meet for lunch to catch up with each other's lives, and made another time months down the road to talk about all our high school friends and share news. From then on almost every year we met near birthday dates. Was this the rerun of the Broadway Play "*Same Time Next Year*" by Bernard Slade? No, simply lunch as past friends, reviving memories, without the affair!

Different perceptions...

What's my purpose in telling you all of this last little entry, besides the joy of telling a light sweet story not drenched with violence, corruption, heavy drama or horrid endings? Our catch up lunch sessions became longer as we had more "retired time". During one of these, we discussed our perceptions of each other in those early teenage years.

It amazed me what information he gave to me about his perception of me, that little insecure, introverted, shy, "afraid to put her hand up", feeling ugly, stupid, less than others, unattractive, clumsy girl! Wow, I was hard on myself as a teenager!

He told me during our high school years, he thought I was fun, smart, had lots of energy and pizzazz, was always coming up with good ideas, didn't let the cliquey girls get to me, had a great body (oh yeah that was mentioned), had great eyes, a way with teachers, was focussed and serious yet fun and frolicky, had a great sense of humour, was a good athlete (what???) and saw me as someone who lived life with purpose. WOW!

I don't know who he was talking about but I let him think it was me! He did however consolidate it by mentioning that he remembered the green polka dot dress I wore most Mondays (yes, apparently I wore it Mondays) and how he thought the scoop neck was rather sexy! I guess it was me he was talking about and I was blown away.

What would be the chances of me looking in a phonebook and discovering someone's name from the past, on the date of their birthday! Many people would just shrug that off as an interesting moment. I felt I needed to act on it! It was a sign of something. In fact I was not in a good space with my marriage at the time and had serious doubts about myself as a person, mother, daughter, sister and wife. This meeting restored my belief in me and what I knew I could be! It reminded me to BE! To be who I was meant to be. Maybe even as the person others saw me as! I still had so many dreams to live.

If only we knew. If only as "doubting" beings who, when we are young, only see what we are missing or how unlike we are to someone else whom we think is luckier, or smarter, or better looking etc.…if only we could see ourselves through someone else's eyes, someone who is not our mother or dad, someone who really sees us objectively…if only. That's the point!

It's never too late to see yourself as you really truly madly deeply are and to celebrate that!!

Being YOU, Being BOLD and BRAVE
can most certainly set you up for living a beautiful vibrant life.

BELIEVE that you can indeed… "boldly go where no one has gone before."
– Captain Picard

Be bold in mind, in body, in what you wish to change, in declaring your plans. Take access to the power of your mind to create audacious bold plans so that you can live in a bold new way! You can actually outgrow your life by boldly stepping out of your comfort zone.

Imagine your comfort zone is a full length zippered hooded coat from head to ankles. Unzip it slowly one zip at a time. Visualize this. See various parts of your mind and body emerging into a world where you are free to be you, free to be bold, free to try out new things, boldly stepping forth to new worlds of being. What an exhilarating feeling it is to discover what's outside your comfort zone!

BE!

Be you! Just be! Slow down. Do the inner work you need to do to create space in your tool kit. Once you have, you can begin to fill it up with bold and brave new tools to bring forth the real authentic badass you really are!

Be BRAVE!

Discover the power your mind can possess when you affirm your intentions to create your dreams. Being BRAVE is about having the courage to be vulnerable even in the presence of fear. When you can feel emotions without letting the emotions control or defeat you, you win! Being brave means moving forward even if you are slightly uncertain. Ask yourself, what is the worst case scenario? Find the "hero" in you. Change into your superhero costume. Come out of the phone booth and emerge Brave and Strong! Heck! Why not? What have you got to lose?

BELIEVE!

"You are what you believe yourself to be!"
- Paul Coelho

What's your own true north in life?

Believe in your dream enough and your heart will finally show you the way.

There are so many more events and incidents in my life that could fill up more books about my adventures on the BOLD brick road, (not necessarily yellow but definitely bold!) whereupon I skipped along merrily, slipping slowly out of my comfort zone to boldly move in a different direction from the one that kept me cozy and unremarkable.

I share with you one more such story. Yes this one too involves the B word 'Boy' yet now I was coming at this as a BODACIOUS BADASS!

Be BODACIOUS!

Single, silly and brazenly bodacious...

Online dating did not yet exist in the mid 1990s when I found myself separated and single. There were only single ads in one column in the newspaper. I hated those ads and refused to put one in the newspaper. Yech, you had to have a special dictionary to figure out all the jargon! (SWF and other abbreviations.) It seemed to me like an entire waste of time. And besides, I really was not looking! Really!

What I did do however, was be creative with my friend Diane, also recently single! Diane was one of those girlfriends everyone needs to have. Envious to all who know her is the fact that no matter how awful life may be, Diane has a way (even more so than me) of finding the silver lining, even when it didn't really look like it was a very polished silver! A great listener, and true to her guidance counselor role in school, Diane was one of those friends that you could rattle on and on and on to, and she would not interrupt (unlike me, in conversations!). When you were finished, she would present you with some truths and make it seem like you were making the decision yourself. In fact what you did was make the decision she already knew you should make! Subliminal messaging was her mantra.

As well, Diane "Queen of Gadgets" is responsible for turning all her friends onto the latest of the latest of "must-haves" for every room in your house, your car, your body, especially your feet, your overall health and much more specifically relating to items that would keep your life super organized. She was into "recommendation" marketing long before you could actually make money doing so. She should have bought stock in Amazon as I am sure she has tripled their income from buyers who normally would not even bother

Three: So B It!

looking at these "thingamajigs". Recently I showed her something for her computer to help with posture and she ordered it. I was thrilled that I actually found something she knew nothing about.

Diane is a great match for my vibration and love of life, for as the "energy bunny" herself, she just does not stop. Together when we travel we make a great team, especially as we are so great at sharing meals! When we peruse a menu, we know automatically what items would work well to order for the both of us. We also share the thrill of being remarkable, arresting, dramatic, noticeable, outright and unmistakable, thus bodacious. As girlfriends in our late 40s, both recently single, we travelled to British Columbia for three weeks and had the time of our life. We loved it so much in Victoria that we made plans to move there and start a business together, a university summer camp experience for elderly seniors who wished to continue to learn and travel.

So while I was not really looking, Diane and I did cook up something we thought would be fun and different. We came up with one of our crazy ideas. We read the singles columns and contacted all the single guys that looked good, some of the single gals from the ads and then included our own single friends inviting them to attend a brunch in Diane's home. All they had to do was bring a potluck item! It was great! There were great breakfast items put on the buffet, everything from bagels and lox to pastries and jujubes. We didn't do anything but provide the place and coffee! We did have some interesting prospects for us (until we realized we were eyeing the same guy), but more or less we simply accumulated many new friends all in the same boat as us. We really should have created a new business. This was all before the many online matchmaker sites. In any case, that was my last attempt to meet someone. I was going solo! I did not need a man! I stood steadfast on that decision. I was getting used to being my own boss! Or so I thought. I was definitely NOT looking. After the brunch event and some very sweet dates with a few gentlemen, with whom I was "fixed up" by good friends, I was now nixing my friend's attempts to continue doing so. I thought I didn't need Prince Charming to make my happy ending! I was finding my own happy place. Until…

March 1996 and a house for sale…

I passed the beautiful house in which I once had dinner with my then-husband, and noticed something unusual. There was a bold red and white "For Sale" sign protruding out of the snowy lawn. This house belonged to my ex's former boss, Rowland, his wife and 3 children. I drove past it every weekday on my way to my school and was always caught by its old English charm! My house was 5 blocks away in North Toronto, an area in which I always dreamed of living.

Four years prior, my then husband and I had downsized our sprawling suburban home for this sweet, unique, thin but tall home in a desired area in Toronto. The size was perfect for us and for the one son whom we thought would live with us only when home from university. Wrong on both counts. The "us" that would spend until old age here was now only ME and my youngest son who was no longer away at university was still living full time with me.

I loved the house, the community, and the fact that I could walk anywhere to get anything I needed or wanted. As I passed by that day, I was indeed curious to find out why Rowland's house was for sale and where he and his family were going? That curiosity drove me down a new bold tunnel, one full of signs and messages from the universe that would change the trajectory of my life. In fact, I surprised myself. It's a story of BOLDNESS and a bit of BADASSERY.

Three: So B it!

The next day when passing by to go home from work, after a bit of shopping, I noticed the house now had a big SOLD sign (that was fast!) and Rowland was just coming out of the house. I slowed down, noticing no car coming either way, rolled down my window and waved, emitting from my face a curious look of puzzlement. He came over to me with a sad smile and explained the situation of his recent separation from his wife. He had just returned with his son from checking out a place to rent a few blocks away. We talked about me and apparently he knew my status, after having had lunch with my ex-husband, his former assistant manager. We chatted a bit more, until we thought it best that I move on should cars come. I started to say goodbye, looked into his eyes and I felt my empathetic heart come into play. I said, "Why don't we have coffee together one day. I just live a few blocks away. I still don't know many people in this neighbourhood and it would be nice to take advantage of one of those new corner coffee shops popping up here and there in our community."

Since being single, I knew personally every Starbucks and Tim's within six blocks. I often went alone to write in my journals or to read, and honestly thought how nice it would be to share time with someone else there. I also truly believed I could help him restore the twinkle in his eye, for it wasn't that long ago that I looked that sad and forlorn. And that was all it was!

He touched my shoulder ever so gently, and I'm not sure what he said in response but his touch said "Sure I'd like that," and my body felt a gentle jolt of electricity that told me this might be more than just a little coffee time. I tried to dismiss this strange feeling because, please remember, my daily mantra was that I did not need a man in my life! But the sizzle could not be denied.

I did not leave a number or address or anything and this was before, cell phones, texts, Instagrams, Messenger etc. Heck, we still had answering machines! I could basically ignore it and let it just go away.

Messages from books...

I have always believed books find you at the right time.

I had just finished reading *Celestine Prophecy* by James Redford and was deep in the belief that there was no such thing as a coincidence; if you have a chance encounter with someone, there is a reason that it happens. You are encouraged to follow the signs (just like the telephone book occurrence with my highschool boyfriend). Redford discusses various psychological and spiritual ideas that are rooted in many ancient Eastern traditions, such as how opening to new possibilities can help an individual establish a connection with the Divine. The main character undertakes a journey to find and understand a series of nine spiritual insights in an ancient manuscript in Peru. The book is a first-person narrative of spiritual awakening. The narrator is in a transitional period of his life and begins to notice instances of synchronicity, which is the belief that coincidences have a meaning personal to those who experience them. This was such a time for me.

I just kept seeing those blue eyes gazing back at me along with the feel of that sweet soft delicate touch that had not yet left me. I was in deep trouble!

Time for a call to a girlfriend! Diane got the call and she listened! My dear friend said it like it is:

"Vivian, for goodness sakes, call him. Set a date and invite him to your house. He is not going to look you up…you are the ex-wife

Three: So B It!

of his assistant area manager with whom he goes to lunch. It's up to you and that's that!"

Just as I resigned myself to do so, I realized that I had forgotten his last name so how could I look up his phone number? Ah, but I could look it up in my son's bar mitzvah album as I know I wrote out all the attendees. Foiled again! I only had their first names. Fortunately I was not ready to give up. I did not know how I would get the number but now I was on a mission. I had full faith that I would find it! Nancy Drew was alive and well! I knew there would be a clue or a sign coming my way.

It came that very night. I was asked to look for a phone number for a friend. I knew it was in an old flip up address book I still had. Found it! Under the D: Dalton. Right underneath this was Rowland's name (spelled incorrectly as Roland) with his last name that started with a D! And so I became brave and called the number presented to me. To no avail. His phone number was not in service. Dialed 411…I had facts! I had details! I had the name and the address! "Sorry, that is a private unlisted number," said the information operator! No Facebook or Linkedin yet available. Now what? I decided that I would wait for business hours. I knew he worked for the government and now knew his full name. I would call Government Services the next day. Whoops! Foiled again! They were on strike!

Would you have given up? I believe in signs. I had a few already. My sense of adventure was with certainty much more powerful than my thoughts of giving up. I was not a quitter!

The next morning I left very late for school, informing the secretary that I had to shovel my driveway out and would be late. Seriously? A major snowstorm in March? Now single, I had to look after this myself. Fortunately, the advantage of being the "principal" of the school meant that I did not have eager eyed students waiting in a classroom and I did have a brilliant Ms. Fix It administrative assistant who, in truth, really managed the school! I drove my usual route on the unplowed city roads much later than usual. Lo and behold Mr. Blue Eyes was out shovelling off the snow from his car. A bit of small talk and my body began to tingle. I call these WATCOs (What are the Chances Of?). I have a whole book of them. This was no longer a chance encounter.

I had moved to the area a few years ago, a few blocks away and had never bumped into him before and now it had happened twice in two days! Now what? Time to go BOLDER with a bit of intentional BADASSERY! I was sizzling with Wonder Woman Vibrations.

My awesome secretary and I devised a note I would leave in his door on the way home from school. This was much more fun than working on the school budget! On my way home, like a nervous jittery highschool girl, I parked the car across the road and ran up to the front door where I slid the note into the mail opening, and flew back to the car, my heart beating out of my chest.

For me that was BOLD and crazy!

I know you want to know what the note said and it just so happens that I kept a copy in my journal. I am embarrassed by my attempt to be so casual:

Three: So B It!

*"Hi Roland (*i.e. Rowland spelled incorrectly*)*

Have you read Celestine Prophecy? If you have, you will know why I am writing to you. There are no such things as coincidences apparently and everything happens for a reason. Interesting that we keep meeting! Would love to have a chat with you over coffee and we can discuss this more in detail. I'm sure we have a lot in common to talk about and upon which to commiserate. Give me a call at ………"

Vivian

Looking at this note, I am surprised that I did not completely scare him away! Now that I know him better, I realize that never in a million years would he have read a spiritual book like *Celestine Prophecy*. What I did find out later is that he did say to himself, after delaying the opening of the note, "Am I really ready for this?" He may still be thinking that!

Three days later he finally called. I had already dismissed my actions as foolhardy. A friend who was going to go to a movie with me that night had just cancelled, letting me know with some irritation that her unreasonable hubby was complaining that she had been out too much that week! It did remind me that I was grateful to be alone and that no man would ever have that kind of control on me again. Nonetheless I was feeling sad and gloomy. The Jewish holidays were approaching soon and I would not see my sons for the family Passover. I was feeling so terribly alone. When the phone rang, I was not expecting it to be Mr. Blue Eyes and so I was thrilled to hear his voice. Had I been out, apparently he would not likely have mustered up the courage again to attempt the phone call. For interfering with my initial plans, I thank my friend's husband!

We talked for ages on the phone until I suggested boldly that since we both had the hockey game on (I lied) why didn't he just come over and watch at my place? He came over certainly not dressed to impress but something excited me. He stayed until 1 AM and our relationship began.

Why do I tell my tale…

Being open to the unexpected leaves room for new paths in your life. To let serendipity do its work and with your quest in mind, you will stumble upon something or someone that might direct you to the right path. You may find a coincidental answer during a phone call with a friend, a conversation with a stranger in a line. Your job is to see it when these moments arrive. BOLDLY embrace serendipity! James Redford, author of *Celestine Prophecy*, teaches:

"The First Insight occurs when we take the coincidences seriously. These coincidences make us feel there is something more, something spiritual, operating underneath everything we do."

and

"You see, the problem in life isn't in receiving answers. The problem is in identifying your current questions. Once you get the questions right, the answers always come."

HEY VIBRANT YOU! IT'S YOUR TURN.
The B Ball is in Your Court

BEING BOLD: Write about one of your bold occurrences.

_____
_____
_____
_____

FEELING BOLD: How did you feel when the boldness came upon you?
List all the adjectives you can think of.

_____
_____
_____
_____

HAVING BELIEF: What's your biggest belief in yourself? How many thoughts can you write here?
I believe I can …

_____
_____
_____
_____
_____

Let's Breathe In and Breathe Out

Find the natural rhythm of your breath

Breathe in Breathe out
Breathe in being confident Breathe out doubt
Breathe in boldness Breathe out insecurity
Breathe in bravery Breathe out fear
Breathe in excitement Breathe out lethargy
Breathe in being!

Now add your own:

Breathe in…	*Breathe out…*
Breathe in…	*Breathe out…*
Breathe in…	*Breathe out…*
Breathe in…	*Breathe out…*

THE B AFFIRMATIONS PAGE

Repeat those that you wish to apply to you today. Say them out loud!

I am a BEAUTIFUL being.
I am BOLD.
I am BRAVE.
I BELIEVE I can accomplish anything I set my mind to doing.

And from my Clubhouse room participants:

I BELIEVE in myself and what I can accomplish.
I keep my BELIEFS intact so I may grow and flourish.
I will live a long life with the BELIEF that I can grow to be the BEST I can be.
BELIEFS BUILD my confidence.
I live a BODACIOUS life by focussing on excellence not perfection.
I BECOME BOLD by stepping up to the plate and on to the playing field.
I am BREEZY carefree and easy as I bring light to any room.
I am BLOSSOMING to become all that I am meant to be.
I live by the mantra BE! BE myself!
I enjoy BEAUTIFUL souls and my loving community.
I am BEAUTIFUL inside and out.
I love BREAKTHROUGHS when I realize I can do anything!
I am always growing, expanding and BLOOMING.

Before ROARING into the next Chapter of Rs, I add one more
B word
in which I encourage you to subscribe:
BADASSERY
Pronunciation /ˈbadasəri/ *noun/ mass noun*
informal North American
behaviour, characteristics, or actions regarded as formidably impressive.

Ready, set, go?
Last affirmation:
I am a BADASS

CHAPTER 5
⭐ Four: ROAR THOSE Rs!
Live Vibrantly by Roaring, Routines & Rituals, Resilience, Radiance, Reflection, Rose-Coloured Glasses & more

Be READY to ROAR

The question is how?
To start and continue to ROAR with the energy you need to live life, you have to take responsibility for your own resurrection and rejuvenation, should you encounter challenges, setbacks or experiences that deviate from where you had planned to be. For me as I matured, I realized that having a spiritual and self-care ROUTINE & RITUAL, specifically in the morning, was something that worked to assist me to be able to pause, breathe and reflect and handle the unexpected.

If you own an electric toothbrush, you know that after prolonged use, all of a sudden, usually right in the middle of brushing, the buzzing will slowly lessen to an inaudible tone and the brushes will just blatantly stop! Luckily you reach into your drawer for the charger, set it up and within a few hours your electric toothbrush is as good as new ready to attack the tartar monsters once again! We need RECHARGERS as well. These come in various forms. Here are the vibrant rechargers I suggest to get back your ROAR when it begins to diminish and possibly stop:

Release to ROUTINES & RITUALS

Growing up with rules…

My mother was the queen of rituals and also rules and rigidity. The rigidity aspect (which I'm afraid to say I did inherit somewhat) was one I decided as a teenager to avoid. I wanted so badly to be low key and accepting of life and how it flowed. My friend in high school, Judy Mack, was such a person. During the mid 60s we were the new age of flower children about to burst forth. I always admired her for her brilliance along with the ability to chill. The last I heard of her she joined a commune in British Columbia.

I hated how rigid my mom was. However I did admire her routines and rituals of organizing the household while working full time, and was amazed at how she practiced self-care. She truly had a way of looking after herself and spent long hours doing her personal self-care rituals, including a lot of private time reading books. Though my love affair with consistent rituals came later in my life, I did get a bit of a grounding in my mid-teens from mama bear, though grizzly she be!

As a young child and teenager, I was very good at manifesting desires, believing I could attract what I wanted and creating vision boards in my mind. At the same time I had no idea how to think better of myself, stay silent to listen to my heart or to write about my thoughts. I continued to live life as a paradox.

FOUR: ROAR THOSE Rs!

I knew I was bright by my marks and what teachers said about me. Unfortunately, I put myself down by convincing myself of how many people were that much brighter than me. I sensed from friends and boyfriends that there was something about me that was attractive, fun and pleasing, yet I was self-critical about my looks and my abilities and went on and on about that to my mom. Self deprecation was a skill of mine. If it were on a report card I would get an A+.

My mother and her friends were constantly praising me for my creative abilities. My mother to her dying day used to always say to me, "What can't you do?" Two of her best friends, one very intellectual and one very social, took me underwing and complimented me regularly while defending me to my mother, who while loving and meaning well, was extremely hard on me.

Inge and Hilde, if you can hear me from your playground in the sky, please know how much I appreciated you.

Despite all this attention, I had no belief in myself, and though my confidence had grown a great deal via my boyfriend days, I had several argumentative discussions with myself. The insecure, inferior, introverted, doubtful, critical side always seemed to win. Fortunately while the mind played tricks on me, the deep-seated thoughts of my soul created my true actions that assisted me as I roared with a RADIANCE, one unbeknownst to me and which always surprised me.

Where there's a will there's a way…

In high school from Grade 10 to Grade 13 I had an incredible German and French teacher, Ms. Will, with whom I had a beautiful loving and academic relationship. She was my inspiration. Another one of my influencers! She changed my life! Her students loved her. We called her "Where there's a Will, there's a way". She was our

Go Vibrant!

Germaine Greer who encouraged women to "define their own values, order their own priorities and decide their own fate".

She recognized in me the need to love myself for every little unique thing about me. She introduced me to a book called *The Power of Positive Thinking* by Norman Vincent Peale, published in 1952. Although the book had many religious connotations, Ms. Will told me to read it for the messages and not the religious aspect as my parents were not Christian. Other than high school texts, I only read fiction, so reading this was no easy task. It was my first real introduction to "self-help" non-fiction. And now here I am writing in this category!

Helen Will was ahead of her time and started me on a ritual of waking up 15 minutes earlier, reading for 10 minutes and then writing for 5 minutes, not about my daily routines or my love interests, as in a secret locked diary, but instead about what I was learning about me. I was to add this starting statement each day and complete the phrase: *Today I am happy that I* ....

I was made to visualize and to affirm myself well before the art of doing so became a "movement".

She gave me a notebook to write in. She invited my girlfriend Judy and me over to her apartment for lemonade occasionally to chat about what we were learning. She discussed the power we had and how women were going to change the world. I loved feeling so special. Our visits were like *Tuesdays with Morrie* or sitting in sessions with John Keating (Robin Williams) of *Dead Poets Society*. We were learning to break out of our shells, pursue our dreams and seize the day.

I kept up that ritual all during my highschool years! But I also kept it fairly secret. Because the book had many references to Christianity I thought my Jewish parents would not approve, while in fact the statements made, other than the connection to Christ, were ones which matched our faith. Basically my ritual of reading and writing helped me with what Mr. Peale was certainly hoping his book would do for youth.

I started to picture myself as succeeding.

I began to think positive thoughts to drown out negative ones.

I overcame obstacles with more intention.

I was learning to love myself yet had a long journey ahead.

I was beginning to develop a stronger sense of self-respect and self-image.

The ritual and routine of writing in the notebook every morning (well not every morning, but I tried!) empowered me way back in 1960 at 15 to start each day loving myself in the battle of trying to conquer my unhealthy self-thoughts.

I have a recollection of Judy and I many years later visiting Ms. Will, who was extremely ill, in a hospital for critical care. We knew it would be our last visit with her. I only hope that she could sense and hear how well we were both doing and how she had changed our lives. I brought my notebook with me to read some pages to her. I think I may have left it there with her.

She was our Dr. Sean Maguire (Robin Williams in *Good Will Hunting*) and we loved her to the moon and back.

After I graduated from secondary school, my university days became super social, crazy active and ridiculously busy trying to achieve my lofty goals. I'm embarrassed and sad to say I gave up my daily rituals for a while but am delighted to say that I did resume them with a vengeance!

Go Vibrant!

Saved by S.A.V.E.R.S....

The good news is that the universe being as it is, brought me back to rituals when I most needed to be reminded of their benefit! I had the pleasure at a business conference of hearing a keynote presentation by Hal Elrod, author of *The Miracle Morning*. I was so moved by his message and his personal story that I immediately jumped into his SAVERS ritual and tried my best to begin my day with the six habits he suggested could help us all on our journey through life.

Since then, I have, as best I can, engaged in this morning ritual with an open mind and open heart. I wake earlier most mornings looking forward to participating in these self-reflection and thoughtful activities, not always in this order:

Silence

A time to calm my overactive busy mind to start my day more purposefully

Affirmations

As in the last page of each of the VIBRANT chapters of this book, I find affirmations help purify my thoughts and translate them into words and then actions. I say affirmations to help me manifest my intentions.

Visualization

When I imagine and paint a picture of something in my mind that directs me to what I wish to achieve, it can become a powerful source of energy to bring about the best version of myself.

Exercise

While not my favorite thing to do, I recognize its importance to my health and longevity. Presently I involve myself in dance, yoga, walking, weight training, and daily flexibility exercises.

Reading

I love to read and am now making more time to envelop myself in the worlds of nonfiction as well as fiction. I am happy to say my repertoire is now much more extensive
than Jackie Collins romance novels or Tom Clancy spy novels.

Scribing

Journalling is my most favourite activity in the ritual. I have over 40 journals that are not just day-to-day records of what I did or what anyone said in return, but great memories of my children's and family's accomplishments, an open window to personal challenges along with my thoughts, feelings and solutions. I now get a sense of pleasure reading them and seeing how I have truly grown with certainly much more to accomplish in that respect.

A well-tended mind, body and soul are mandatory when it comes to our ability to show up in healthy ways for ourselves and others and give with abundance. You do not necessarily have to subscribe to the ritual or routine that is working for me. I highly recommend that you find a ritual that works for you, even if it means waking up one hour earlier or forgoing watching the news or one more binged episode of a Netflix season. You are the most important thing of the day! If you do not have a consistent routine, try it! You will thank you!

Have RESILIENCE

The birth of my resilience …

In the summer before Grade 6, we moved and once again I found myself in a new school, new class, new classmates. To make matters worse, my new teacher, while everyone sitting in rows was completing their Math assignment, called me to his desk. In front of him was the OSR file in which every teacher I ever had in my prior five years, starting at kindergarten, had written comments about me in a little section indicating the grade. This file passes on from one teacher to the next. The stern looking Mr. Sanders was no exception. Most of it that I could see was glowing except for one comment made by my former Grade 5 teacher. I remember it as if it was yesterday. Mr. Sanders read this out loud to me in a booming voice that could be heard three classrooms down. These were his words:

> MR. S: Vivian, welcome to the class. Do you know what this is?
> *(Nod from my head)*
> Do you see what it says here?
> *(Second nod)*
> Let me read it for you to make sure.
> "*Vivian is a smart, hardworking student but tends to disturb and distract the work of others. She needs to curb her talkativeness.*"
> I want you to understand that this kind of behaviour WILL NOT, shall I repeat…will not…be tolerated in this classroom. Do you understand?
> *(Third nod)*
> You can go back to your seat now.

He may well have just sent me to the guillotine or to be burned at the stake! He had completely screwed my chances of being in a bully-free environment or having friends in this new school. As if my insecurities weren't already taking shape, I was mortified.

Shamefaced, hurting inside, and shocked, somehow I wrapped myself tightly in a protective shroud that prevented me from crying as I walked back to my seat. I did so walking straight, strong and tall. I told myself that he had not won even a small percent of any of the admiration and love I had had for my former teachers. He did however cause my competitive spirit to rise! I convinced myself that I would show him! It was the first time I had sprung back with such vitality. It was the birth of my RESILIENCE! I surprised myself because I was very sensitive and cried easily. This day was a red letter day for me.

I knew it would be hard to stop talking. I always finished my work early and there was nothing to do but wait for "answer" time. To quiet the boredom, I would talk to my nearby classmates. I promised myself that I would try to curb my enthusiasm. Instead of being angry, I would show that Mr. Sanders! I vowed I would impress him with my grades. And that I did! My Grade 6 year was my best year ever in the A+ category! I showed him alright.

My classmates? I was prepared for the worst, already envisioning the excuses I would make to my parents that I was too sick to go to school. However, for the most part my new classmates were surprisingly empathetic. I think they all disliked Mr. Sanders. I had that going for me. For some strange reason, instead of teasing me for the remark he made, it was as if they were rooting for the underdog, that being me. A few girls came to me at recess offering me playtime and friendship. That was good enough for me. I breathed in and even though I didn't even know the word resilient yet, I felt it!

Go Vibrant!

On occasion I was still sent to the cloakroom for talking! I just couldn't help it! School back then did not make accommodations for those who needed more challenges or finished their work before others. Perhaps I was A.D.D., or whatever label they would have given me in those days. I simply could not sit still waiting for the time Mr. Sanders deemed it to be "Take Up" time! I swore to myself that if I ever became a teacher, I would have areas in the hall that kids could go to when they finished their work to engage in extra interesting activities. This was long before "group" and independent learning!

I didn't mind standing in the cloakroom for 15 minutes! It gave me something to do. And I was not teased about it as I was at my other school. I would take a little notebook and create doodles and drawings to ease the wait back to class. I also used this at my desk when I finished my work too fast! My friends loved it when I shared with them my cloakroom graffiti pages! They admired my creativity. I recall many drawings of Mr. S yelling at the class. Luckily he never saw them.

Where were my parents in all this? They of course asked me about my first day of school. When I told them both at dinner that night, sobbing uncontrollably, I thought they would coddle me a bit! Nope! My mother spoke to my father in German and said "*Vielleicht lernt sie es jetzt. Sie wird darüber hinwegkommen!*" which basically translates to: "Maybe now she'll learn. She'll get over it!" Tough broad, my mom! I attribute to her my empowerment to develop resiliency.

My dad, when kissing me goodnight, whispered: "Be strong Vivichen. I hope you have a better day tomorrow!" He was my number one fan. Often that year, when he knew I had a bad day, he loved looking at and adding his own artwork and fancy lettering to my cloakroom book that I named "Creative in the Cloakroom".

Four: Roar Those Rs!

I dreamt of this book one day being displayed boldly in the Coles bookstore in our local mall. I would dedicate it to all the children like me who were sent in isolation, simply because they finished their work! Had I even known that I was being resilient or known what the word resilient meant, I would have named it "Room for Resilient Responses".

Resilience after being naive…

In May 1967 my girlfriend Sharon W. and I were ready to slay and conquer the world! Not many of our girlfriends had gone to University and a few we know were only out to get their MRS degree. We had mastered our Bachelor of Arts! Really that was a big deal back then! I had to give up my grandiose dreams of being a United Nations translator, as I received a PWH (Pass Without Honours) in my first year of my 4-year honour course Modern History and Modern Languages. (You may remember how I felt about History!) My young age and immaturity caught up to me as did my social life versus my academic studies. I did not realize at the time, the PWH meant I just could not continue in the Honours course and I could transfer to 2nd year General Arts. Not knowing this, I bounced back from the news of my failure (which is what I thought it was), to looking forward to a whole new beginning in First Year General Arts, with Psychology as my major, and that's where I met my bestie Sharon W. Things happen for a reason!

I met Sharon W. (then Sharon E.) in her first year of university, (my second), as we shared a table in our assigned Psychology lab. It happened that she shared a number of classes with me and it did not take long for us to be fast friends. Her great sense of humour and wit would crack me up when lectures got boring and we would make the class fun with our own interpretations of what the lecturer was actually pontificating about. It may well have been the reason the Sociology professor violently threw a piece of chalk at my head, which he followed up with a childish tantrum. True story! Back to our mutual friendship, in exchange, Sharon loved my meticulous and organized note taking which I was happy to lend her.

We did not live far from each other and car-pooled together to and from U of T with some guy named George who probably regretted being with us two ditsy giggly non stop talking girls especially during heavy traffic! We both did well in university and I attribute this to our unique way of studying together for exams. We would figure out possible questions that would be on the finals and create interviews, musicals, poems, and theatre shows that would give the answers! Sharon's living room became the venue for us to practice and rehearse. We were hysterical! We spent more time breaking into laughter then actually studying, however, it worked! I just had to remember not to sing out loud when writing the exam!

Now that we had graduated with flying colours, degree in hand, we decided that everyone was waiting to hire us! Armed with our resumes, portfolios and the naive confidence of new graduates, we set out to enter every building in the business section of Toronto. We knew without a doubt that there were CEOs out there ready to hire us in a nanosecond! For what, I don't know. We just assumed they would be so happy to have women with a Bachelor of Arts Psychology Major in their firm. Didn't every office want one of us?

When the best offer that day was a file clerk position at minimum wage, a job I had done as a summer student, we realised our expectations had deceived us! Needless to say, dejected and embarrassed, we went to my home with our tails between our legs. We knew we had to be resilient! Now I knew what the word meant! We knew we could not give up hope. For some reason, we had such a strong belief that

FOUR: ROAR THOSE Rs!

we were meant to do more, be more, achieve more and that the path would somehow open up to us.

We scoured the papers and there it was! A large half page black and white ad staring us in the face. I swear it was actually calling out to us! "The Ontario College of Education is looking for students with university degrees to attend O.C.E. in Toronto and get a degree in teaching, along with a bursary of $500 if you apply and are accepted!" A college that pays you money to attend classes? Unheard of!

Neither Sharon and I had thought of being a teacher. If you recall, my childhood desire was to be principal and bypass the teacher role. I really wasn't sure of this move. And neither of us knew whether we were suited for elementary or secondary or any teaching role for that matter. No problem! They were offering a course that included both options and we chose the mixed program with Art and English as my high school majors. Practice teaching was divided up between high schools and elementary schools. Imagine my history teacher, Mrs. Gillette's surprise when I showed up in the staff room of my former high school where I was assigned one of my practicums! I told her "Don't worry Mrs. G. I'm not here to teach history". She was thrilled for me!

As it happened we both fell in love with teaching. It was meant to be and we were both darn good at it! We were so fortunate to secure fantastic jobs in two amazing schools and later both of us were promoted to vice principal and then principal! I loved every minute of helping and being rewarded by watching young people grow. Later as a leader of the school, I reveled in the impact I was able to make in the school community with parents, staff and students. I delighted in watching adult teachers grow into the role they were meant to play, making a difference in the lives of youth. There was no room for any "Mr. Sanders" in my schools.

GO VIBRANT!

To this day, Sharon and I are still the best of friends. We marvel and laugh now at our resilience over 50 years ago that allowed us to bounce back and switch mindsets so quickly and determinedly! And we know now it was meant to be!

As I age, I realise that I have to be more and more RESILIENT than ever before. I wrote this poem a couple of years after my separation and keep it close to me. I read it often when I am in a funk, feel low, need a change and desperately need that spoonful of resilience!

MOVING ON THROUGH TEARS

Release the tears and let them flow
Tears hold the tales, tears let them go
Don't be afraid, don't hold them back
Tears cry inside for what we lack
They're nature's hands to aid you through
Guiding, cleansing, helping you
With relentless pain. Will it cease?
Tears lead you forth to clouds of peace
Cry angry tears out one by one
Set free them all until they're done
Shed tears of sadness, let them flow
Breathe again, survive and grow
Dance once again! Pirouette once more!
For you've survived your personal war
Resilient now . The trauma freed
Fly now to where you are meant to be!

Vivian Shapiro - Jan 13 1996

FOUR: ROAR THOSE Rs!

Release RADIANCE

Why me? This is beyond a doubt one of my all time favourite stories. It was also the ultimate answer to a question I had asked myself countless times. For a large part of my life, at various events, parties, functions, and plays, out of the blue, I was often asked as an audience member to come and join the performers on stage, no matter where I was sitting or happening to be.

To my surprise and often embarrassment, among the many times I could list, I have been…

- *led by the hand to be a dance partner with the "Phantom" of the Opera while he serenaded me with "The Music of the Night"*
- *asked to assist a magician*
- *called up to be part of an improv comedy team on cruises and at Club Med shows (many times)*
- *brought on stage with The Jersey Boys at an off-Broadway performance*
- *invited on stage to be courted with The Altar Boys in a community theatre production*
- *selected to be part of a dance team on stage*
- *coerced to perform "You know You Make Me Wanna Jump" with a Blues Brothers group*
- *surprised to receive the one pink silk scarf given to an audience member from the Elvis impersonator*
- *kidnapped by thieves on horses in a shootout western scene set-up at a conference in the Yukon*

Why me? The list is endless. Never once did I volunteer, raise my hand or shout "Me! Me! Me! Pick me!" This next story is by far my most memorable experience and answers "Why Me?"

A magical, musical, mystery tour is coming to take me away!

In May 2013, Rowland and I attended the annual 4 day conference run by the U.S. National Alcohol Beverage Control Association (NABCA) for which he was a Canadian delegate. A bonus for me, as I was able to attend each year. Walking into the plenary session at the Arizona Biltmore grandroom, we were curious to know why the usual seats that would be set up theatre style in straight rows one behind each other, were arranged quite differently. The seats meant for participants were now placed oddly, in a semicircle, in-between and around chairs that already had musical instruments placed on them. It was very confusing but we placed ourselves between some wind instruments on one side and wood on the other, instead of sitting right next to the usual delegates of the conference. I felt as if we were in for an immersive experience and was truly excited!

Maestro Roger Nierenberg from New York entered the room, along with an entire professional symphony orchestra. The musicians took their seats integrated amongst the delegates. As they did, each one started tuning up their instruments while we watched in fascination sitting virtually next to them. "The Music Paradigm" presentation is one in which the maestro leads the audience through fascinating musical dynamics to reveal what makes organizations excel and what may cause dysfunction. Using the orchestra and a conductor as the analogy of a company and its leaders, he had the audience spellbound as they clearly adapted to the similarities.

And that's when he called me up to the stage. I had no warning. The maestro did not ask for a volunteer. The conference committee

Four: Roar Those Rs!

had not fixed it. No! He simply looked at me about 15 rows back and asked me to join him on stage. And that's when my hubby also received a phone call to which he had to attend and grudgingly left the room. I sheepishly walked up the steps and faced the musicians and the audience. I am sure the many delegates who knew me, including the CEO were saying to themselves: "Yup, here goes Viv again!" This was getting embarrassing!

The experience I had was indescribable. Maestro Nierenberg continued the presentation, engaging me and the audience to give observations to insights that could be applied to strengthen their organizations. But this time, after receiving a brief lesson on rhythmically moving and holding a baton, I, little ol' me, became the conductor! I led at first with his gentle guidance of his hand on mine, bringing in the full orchestra or certain sections as instructed. And then I was on my own with only verbal directions as he continued to demonstrate various musical situations while engaging the audience. It was surreal. It was magic. (And it didn't hurt that this conductor was pretty darn handsome.)

And Rowland? He was not even there to experience it! (or take photos!)

When the session was over, as the Maestro was leaving I went over to personally thank him for choosing me and to tell him how very special the experience was. At that point in time, I was convinced that Jim Squeo, President and CEO of NABCA, or his staff had something to do with my selection so I asked Roger. (We were now on a first name basis!) He responded: "Absolutely not. I knew myself that you would be the right person to take on the task!" I asked him how he knew. He responded, "That, my dear, is because when I look into the audience I look for someone who shines their radiance, revealing their interest with a luminosity, and that was you!" Wow!

And how did I do that? I only know that I give my undivided attention to such presentations, I show my pleasure, I smile a lot and I absorb the stories so that I feel the moment. That's it! I never knew that radiance can emit rays for others to see or feel. I now know! The formula is simple!

In the evening, we roamed around the kiosks organized by companies proudly displaying and presenting their wines, liquors or liqueurs hosting their booze brands. This was the fun part. Delegates congratulated me for an outstanding performance and I was greeted with many "Bravo Maestra!" accolades. Quite the day and night!

Go out there and radiate your RADIANCE and you too may find something special awaiting you!

Reflect on Self

Self REFLECTION which may be part of the RITUALS you perform, is also a habit stacking exercise on its own. Practice this daily.

1. Choose to be honest with yourself,
2. Notice your behaviour patterns and determine your areas for growth,
3. Know your true you and determine your core values to evaluate how you carry those out,
4. Be forgiving and kind to yourself when you go off the path,
5. Record your own observations and personal development successes in a journal.

Four: Roar Those Rs!

Use Rose-Coloured Glasses

"She sees the world through rose-coloured glasses
Painted skies and graceful romances
I see a world that's tired and scared
Of living on the edge too long
Where does she get off telling me
That love could save us all
Save us all"
- "Rose-Coloured Glasses" by Blue Rodeo

Which one are you? Do you see the painted sky and graceful romances or are you dragged down by watching our tired and scary world with a fearsome, anxious mind? I refuse to hide from the vibrancy our world and fellow dwellers have to offer.

While I may have misplaced those glasses once in a while, losing myself to the overpowering negativity that may prevail at the time, I soon find my way back to my rosy retrospection. I have often been teased about the way I view the world as an optimist, through these rose-coloured glasses, through my "positive peepers". I have been chastised in fact with comments that I am unrealistic. Whatever it may be, it satisfies my need for living with happiness, joy and vibrance. And I have learned to listen to me, not others.

Seeing the world through rose-coloured glasses, seeing things in a positive light can actually improve our lives. Expecting the best possible outcome of events often leads to just that! Research shows that shifting one's attention away from toxic emotions produces better mental health.

As I emphasize often at the end of many of my chapters: Try it, you will like it!

GO VIBRANT!

HEY VIBRANT YOU!! IT'S YOUR TURN
Ready Set Go!

1. Set your clock for 5 minutes. (You may need to get your own piece of paper for this.) In non-stop fashion, keep your pencil moving, not lifting it from the paper. Write down all the ways you have been resilient so far in life. Surprise yourself! Ready Set Go!

   _____
   _____
   _____
   _____
   _____
   _____
   _____
   _____
   _____
   _____

2. Find a pink or red crayon or marker for this next task. Artist or not, draw your face here in pen or pencil. Use the pink marker and, as best you can, place over your eyes, the sexiest, boldest, funkiest pair of rose coloured glasses that you can imagine! Now complete the sentence on the next page:

FOUR: ROAR THOSE Rs!

REFLECTION

I see myself and the world through rose coloured glasses.
I create who I am and I am vibrant!

I do this by...

_____
_____
_____
_____
_____

MY RITUALS

I have certain routines I do to create focus and well being
so I may live with purpose and roar my genius

Rituals I presently subscribe to:

_____
_____
_____
_____
_____

New rituals I wish to add:

_____
_____
_____
_____
_____

A Roaring R Reminder to REST

My final Roaring R word, which I have to constantly remind myself to do, is to find time to REST. Without rest, conscious rest, basically ordering myself to rest, I could not nearly be able to keep vibrant, vivacious, vital and vigorous. Yes I do love alliteration!

In today's world especially, where we are presently acting out of fear of the unknown in our present "covid" mindset and facing more stressful situations of life itself, rest remains a true antidote for better health. If you are anything like me, you have allowed your life to be busy, solving problems day in and day out. I admit, I get so wrapped up with "doing" that I forget to rest!

Even though I know I should, I make choices not to rest. I avoid rest, just to get things done.

So before we enter the R affirmations and soar to the A Star, for me specifically and for you expressly, here is my alliteration attempt which I now have posted for me to see daily!

ROARING "R" REMINDER TO REST

Remember to Rest!
Respect my Requirement to Rest.
Rest will Refuel, Refresh, Reignite, Refill, & Reenergize me.
Rest will Reap Resounding Results to Recover and Restore all of me
Rewiring my body, mind and soul.
Really!

THE R AFFIRMATIONS PAGE

Repeat those that you wish to apply to you today. Say them out loud.

I ROAR with RADIANCE and light up a room.

I take RESPONSIBILITY for showing up big.

I REJUVENATE myself with exercise and fresh air.

I know what tools to use to RECHARGE my energy when necessary.

I practice ROUTINES and RITUALS that serve me well.

I am RESILIENT in the face of adversity or challenges, learning from my hard times.

Everything is RIGHT about me!

I practice self REFLECTION to better myself.

I allow myself to see the world through ROSE coloured glasses.

I give myself permission and find time to REST without guilt.

CHAPTER 6
★ Five : Ace the As

Get Vibrant through Actions, Adventures, Achievements, Audacity, Abundance, and an Attitude of gratitude

LIGHTS CAMERA ACTION: THE BEGINNING

"But let no person say what we could or could not do since we are not judges of ourselves 'til circumstances force us to action."
- Abigail Adams

To lead a *VIBRANT* life, I encourage you to be *ACTION* oriented.

Action leads to Adventures.
Adventures lead to Achievements.
Achievements no matter how big or small attract others and events into your life.

In the words of motivational speaker Jim Rohn:
"You are the average of the five people you spend the most time with."

Take ACTION

In stressful times

March 23 2020: my life partner drove me to the hospital to be tested for coronavirus. It was pretty traumatic. Full lockdown in Toronto was just around the corner and my symptoms were pretty scary…fever, dry cough, chest hurting, out of breath. I had just returned from Mexico and then immediately went up north to a resort in Ontario where 200 youth and their teachers would be hosted for our 14th annual Future: A Conference Empowering Self 2020 Leadership Retreat.

Personal exhaustion always came with co-managing with my good friend and business partner, Amanda, this six day event of sleepless nights. The pre-conference training and preparation for the delegates, the on-call 24-7 management of the 3-day overnight event, ensuring the safety and wellness of over 150 youth aged 12 to 16 was exhilarating but took its toll. During the post-conference responsibilities I could feel the stress on my body, packing up the van, lugging the materials back to the office, and finally making it back home where I crashed. Please know, while I knew there would be a price to pay, I loved every minute knowing we were changing lives.

Every year I ended up with a bad cold that usually brought on ugly congestion and a week at home with at least two days in bed. This year seemed different. It was now more than two weeks and coronavirus symptoms seemed to be looming on the horizon. Rowland did the responsible thing. He phoned the Health Line number. He was told to take me immediately to the nearest hospital. I was tested with a quick scan. My high blood pressure and crackly cough was enough in the early days to put me in isolation in a closed room surrounded by glass. As the parade of nurses and doctors with worried looks came

FIVE : ACE THE AS

in and out of my room, administering one test after another, including the nasal deep and wide intrusion soon to be known as the PCR, I could not help but be worried. As I watched I had such admiration for these front line workers who in those early days came into my room dressed like Star Wars storm troopers. After vacating the room, they shed their face shields, white robes, protective armour and white gloves and disposed of them. To re-enter, they donned a completely new sanitized costume. It was pretty frightening. All I was missing was the IMAX screen.

After chest and back X-rays and more tests, I was sent home to isolate until I would receive the results. I went home masked in the back seat of our car. Poor Rowl had been waiting outside for 2 hours and upon entry into our house I moved into the guest bedroom. I was told it would take up to 10 days! Yes I was worried, nervous and scared. One thing however was clear to me. When free and cleared of this dreaded virus, if in fact that was what I had, I would take *ACTION* to help others. I wasn't sure what I would do. I WAS certain I would do something! The world was crying out for help. No one was hearing it yet!

Taking ACTION is a way to keep *VIBRANT*, especially if it's *ACTION* that helps others!

By the time my negative results came in, the coronavirus was moving full steam all over the globe and through my city, with record numbers of positive cases and many deaths specifically with seniors. First Responders were over-extended and working long hard hours trying to help those hospitalized. Many of my grandchildren were doing virtual online learning, isolation was the name of the game and I couldn't stop thinking of my friends who were single and had no one with whom to isolate. (Although many months later living

Go Vibrant!

24/7 with the same person, one tends to wonder who might have been better off!)

When deciding what ACTION to take I asked myself these questions in an ACRONYM for ACTION. I do love my acronyms as you are beginning to notice I am sure.

What could I do that would be….

    A   AFFIRMING AN ATTITUDE OF GRATITUDE?
    C   CHILD centred?
    T   TEACHABLE?
    I   INSPIRING?
    O   OPTIMISTIC?
    N   NURTURING to others?

And so… I opened myself up to those possibilities…to take action with those goals in mind.

Actions to affirm an attitude of gratitude

I decided to collect and create images of the community support and love occurring during the coronavirus crisis (which unfortunately at the time of this writing, the virus is still creating havoc). My vision was to create a Youtube video that could be sent out via a number of virtual platforms to give hope to our communities. The song I had created 20 years ago with singer-songwriter Richard Samuels called "Sharing a Dream" (see Chapter 2) had the perfect message to provide the background for these pandemic portraits.

Here it is for you to enjoy and bring calm to relieve any fear and anxiety that, as I write this, still exists. I dedicate this as a tribute and remembrance of how our communities bonded to support one another!

https://youtu.be/WhDi6K_7v-E

Or look for it on my youtube channel: Vivian Shapiro

Actions to create something child-centred and teachable

I worried about my youngest school-aged grandson Sawyer, who at age 4 would be missing out on one of the most important times of social interaction with his peers: Junior Kindergarten! His teacher ran a magnificent Virtual Online program but I thought we could do even more to engage students and teach them more about following COVID guidelines and just have some fun! We created together *"The Vava and Sawyer Show"* which we did on Zoom and I used Vimeo to record each one. We invited guests both children and adults. We did over 40 episodes. One time his whole class came on! Sawyer became the idea person and we even had virtual planning time together. We created an opening number song, ending song, a song about washing hands and a very cute teaching song about "coronavirus". This was a great way of bonding with my grandson in a time of isolation, while being part of those precious years of him being 4 and 5! The show was well received by young parents with bored children at home!

Teaching Scribing with Sawyer
https://youtu.be/IYkA4ImH05o

The CoronaVirus Rock for Kids
https://youtu.be/hJSbT8JDLYI

Actions to inspire optimism and nurturing

Most of my friends were fortunate to have a spouse, a roommate or even adult children living with them during this TIME OUT period. My compassion was for those who would be alone, no office, no social life, no one with whom to have real conversations, no dating, no eating out, no parties etc, but hallelujah, we could Zoom! I wish I had bought stocks in the company.

Huggers from a Distance (well before Clubhouse) was a Tuesday and Thursday hourly Zoom opportunity I created with my spiritual friend Miriam as an open forum for those who wished to engage with friends and strangers on set topics fancifully conceived by us. I sent out an invitation to everyone I knew that might be feeling alone or lonely and then all the others whom I thought would enjoy this sort of thing. It did the trick. Although I knew everyone, at first most were strangers to each other, but we all soon got to feel a sense of camaraderie and fun when we met twice a week. As a plethora of Zoom interest groups, operas, book clubs, discussion groups, theatre, museum etc. soon appeared, we wound down to once a week and soon we knew we could move on to other interests. I felt good that my lonely friends felt less alone for those two days of the week! We focused on laughs and topics of support. We all felt as if we were going through an adventure together. We needed those hugs especially from a distance!

We cannot guarantee success but we can deserve it!

ACTIONS lead to ADVENTURES and to ACHIEVEMENT

ACHIEVE and ACCOMPLISH !

And the winner is...

… Vivian Shapiro from Park Lawn Public School! How I remember the incredulous feeling that came over me at the age of 10! This was my first real memory of an achievement. The step ladder the caretaker helped me position at the doorway so students entering the auditorium needed to choose to go under or squeeze in between the door frame and the ladder, was a great lead into my opening line of my public speaking speech, "Superstition Mysteries". I was now able to compete against all other winners from Ontario. This was huge for me. I felt so accomplished and ready for anything coming my way. Even though I did not win the Ontario Championship, this small feat was a taste of what it was like to be successful. And I wanted more!

"Who you are tomorrow begins with what you are today." - Tim Fargo

No achievement, no accomplishment is too small to help recognize your skills and abilities. What is your first memory of an achievement that made you proud of you? It's important for all of us to concentrate on those accomplishments that helped us along our life's journey rather than focusing on what did not succeed. Be the vibrant cheerleader for your own life!

HEY VIBRANT YOU! IT'S YOUR TURN
The Write Stuff...

You are invited to apply to be a contestant on the show
So You Think You Can Achieve!

TURN PAGE FOR YOUR APPLICATION ▶▶▶

Have you ever listed your achievements in life so far? Maybe you have had to write a resume for an interview or job application. Those are formal and objective oriented. Boring! We are looking for more, much more!

Our show is dedicated to honouring those who have taken action to achieve all sorts of crazy badass things that make them who they are today, over and above their career. To apply for the show you are asked to list any achievement you have made in your life no matter how big or small, something that made you proud of you? Let go of all modesty!

BRAG about you and just BRING IT ON!

No achievement is too small or seemingly insignificant to share so we can celebrate you.

Start here:

I ……………………….., proudly drop all modesty as I celebrate these achievements and accomplishments!

_____
_____
_____
_____
_____
_____
_____
_____
_____
_____
_____
_____
_____

FIVE : ACE THE As

_____

_____

_____

_____

_____

_____

_____

_____

My Application

Yes of course I applied also! I decided it would be fun to try and dig out all those things I did that were different, where **action was my guide and achievement was my result.** Here are a few. Each has a special longer story, in this or other chapters in here or maybe for a second book!

> I, Vivian Shapiro, proudly drop all modesty
> as I celebrate these achievements & accomplishments!

lyricist and co-writer of popular songs: "Between Friends" actually made it to the top 20 on BMI charts and what a thrill it was to hear it regularly on the radio (that's what we listened to in those days!), as well as in malls, in a grocery store on their music systems or hearing the very talented singer-songwriter Richard Samuels sing it live at the downtown Toronto piano bar.

co-creator of Flash de Soto and the Champions, a 50s/60s singing group that took an irreverent look at the Toronto District School Board practices, specifically about principal issues and we performed with a select group of administrators, at conferences and much more (true story under AUDACIOUS). We even created a spinoff of SNL called *Thursday Night Live* and an interactive Murder Mystery involving the top brass of our board. When bigwigs retired from the school board we were approached to do retirement events and all of us were excited except Bruce who knew that we couldn't really sing (all but one) and how much work would be involved for us both! I loved it! Bruce learned to love it, though he would never admit it!

writer of children's books which I really should get published. One is based on my eldest son's concern about overnight camp, "Should I Go, I Don't Know", and the other published in-house to give to schools, based on the story of Herbert H. Carnegie entitled "A Friend Called Attitude". Herb is in the I Chapter.

co-creator, original plays, songs for schools such as Lillian Street Public School's school song for its 100th year Centennial celebration, the Millenium play and much more.

artistic director, performer and assistant choreographer, 17 years, for "Cabaret Singers", a group of wannabes from the school board who wanted to sing, act and perform for colleagues, friends and family. Our amazing production team created an annual three-night show that actually impressed our invited guests!

becoming a school principal in the days when it was male-dominated. I believe one of my greatest accomplishments actually as it was quite early in the game for women.

being a wedding officiant in Los Angeles for my friend's son's wedding

empowering young people as the Future Aces Education Director. This achievement is one in which worlds collided through the law of attraction which resulted in making such a huge difference for others.

receiving awards such as the Waterfront Toronto Philanthropy Award and the ACE Award for my work servicing and helping youth

winning contests: best bathing suit contest 1999 …me 50+ against 20 year olds! Prize: Tequila! and various jive contests, also rewarded with booze! It's all about getting the right dance partner! (Thx Neil)

FIVE : ACE THE AS

Live AUDACIOUSLY

You cannot be what you can't see

Living vibrantly is living AUDACIOUSLY, that is, simply living yourself, out loud and bold. Yes I know I have already been bold in the B chapter. Audacious is a little bit above bold. Please know, Audacious is not a bad word! It requires almost a sort of restlessness, a daring move, being a risk taker, being fearless to fulfill dreams that you may have already envisioned, but that you may have resisted!

How to be Audacious? Simple! See the possibilities. Don't hesitate! As Nike says: "JUST DO IT!"

Audacious me as a young teacher

I was just 28 and back to my teaching career three months after giving birth to my second son. My principal John Mclean saw something in me that I wasn't ready to see. He visited my classroom and after dismissing the eager students ready to hurry out for recess, he stayed to tell me he was preparing me for my interview for administrator. Say what?

I was flattered but I told him that I did not have that ambition and how much I loved being in the classroom, loving all my students. John gave me that little sneaky smile of his that told me he had an agenda. He explained to me that I may say that now, yet as I make my impact, he knows that in time I will want to have a greater significance in the educational world. His wise words: "In the classroom you have an impact on 30 students. As a leader in an elementary school you will have an impact on 30 plus staff all having an impact on 30 students. And if you want to go higher, imagine the impact you will have then. I see this in you. I see this for you. Humour me! If anything, you will learn the process and possibly it will be a path you will wish to take when choosing your future teaching journey." He convinced me to try and promised me his coaching and training. I have always been so fortunate to have had very supportive and mentoring principals both as a teacher, convener and vice principal. With John's help, I prepared as best I could.

The day came. Forty percent of those who applied apparently made it to this interview. I was one of a very few women and certainly no one as young as me. I was so out of my league!

This was 1973 when the gentleman's club was alive and well in the North York Board of Education. I was greeted by a trim young petite secretary who asked me to have a seat outside the conference room and in her sweet little lilting voice, she asked me if I was OK and did I need something? Yes! I needed to find the exit!

When I was led inside I was a mass of sweat and was cursing John Maclean. Three men were sitting at a rectangular table with Mr. Markovitch, whom I knew as a superintendent. He was the one who had greeted me seven years prior at the teacher hiring session. I knew one other principal. The other two seemed ready for retirement. Mr. M asked me if I wanted a cup of tea.

Really? A cup of tea? I remember wondering if that's what he offered the male candidates or was there a case of beer hidden somewhere? Perhaps Ms. Sweet Lilting Voice had suggested tea for the women. I said yes, but immediately regretted it when the delicate cup and saucer began to shake in my hand. Aha I thought…the first test! The "Can-she-talk-with–a-full-cup-of tea-in-her-hand?" test! I sat down and never touched the tea again for the whole interview.

The questions began. John had prepared me better than well. I was able to answer all the questions with confidence, and I actually surprised myself! Then came the final question.

MR. MARKOVITCH: Well Mrs. Shapiro you certainly have impressed us. I have one more question: What does your husband feel about your aspirations?

Are you ready for my first discovery of audacity? My audacity?
The thoughts that flashed before me were not nice. Did they ask the men how their wives felt? I didn't hesitate to answer and when I did so, I actually could not believe it was me!

ME: Thank you for that question, Mr. Markovitch. He is extremely supportive and excited for me, as I imagine your wife was for you when you had those aspirations! And all of those of you on this panel!

He smiled, thanked me very much and escorted me out to a lovely smile awaiting for me from Ms. Sweet Lilting Voice, with whom I later became really good friends when we both moved up in our positions, her as the administrative assistant to my family superintendent!

"Bravo for you," remarked John McLean as I told him the whole story of my interview, thinking if ever I did want to be a principal, my career had ended with that last remark. "Absolutely not. You just made yourself well remembered by those four interviewers as a bold mover and shaker!", John acknowledged. How did he know that? His friend on the interviewing team called him after the interview. And Mr. Markovitch? He became a fan of mine!

I thank my audacious younger self.

Audacious me as a newly promoted Vice Principal

Thirteen years later, the time was right for me. I felt the desire to create a bigger wave, a larger splash, as John McLean said I would. Veronica Lacey, Women's Affirmative Action Consultant, and Superintendent Marguerite Jackson encouraged women to take the new leadership courses available to those seeking promotion. As well they hosted sessions with women with career aspirations (who did not necessarily need a husband's support). It was a marvelous time. Women leaders were feeling so appreciated and affirmed. I will forever be grateful for the support of these forward thinking women, who both became Directors of Education!

After going through the many hoops, so different from the first panel interview, I was shortlisted and received a promotion to Vice Principal in 1985. In fact, Marguerite Jackson, Superintendent of Schools that year, was responsible for my placement in her family of schools and became a true mentor, advisor, supporter and, even more importantly, a very good friend to this day.

Becoming a school administrator was a great accomplishment, however, the audacious me, now in this position, accomplished something much more brassy! Read on!

The Birth of Flash De Soto and the Champions

In the fall of my first year in the position of Vice Principal of Bayview Elementary Middle School, I attended my first ever 3 day 2 night North York Principals' Association Conference as a full fledged rookie! The ratio of administrator women to administrator men was outstandingly low given that there were 80 percent women teachers in elementary classrooms compared to 20 percent men.

As far as socialization amongst colleagues, for us new to the scene, especially the new females on board, we were good to look at, but conversations, especially professional ones, were fairly limited. My proud papa bears did make it a point to engage me, all seemingly very happy to see me promoted as their protégé, each principal (all men) probably assuming it was due to their mentorship that I was there!

For the most part when it came to dinner and the later entertainment scheduled for Saturday night, the newbies clustered together on two of the round tables set out. We were a lively young group not deterred by the old school traditions, the cliques or the male climate. We were out to make our mark and change the climate and world of education in our schools. We were pumped and thrilled to be in a position of leadership.

As dinner ended and the room was getting set for the entertainment, a very strange scene occurred. Over half the room of male principals disappeared. Now I know some of them looked old, but surely they weren't calling it a night already? Wrong! It was a tradition on Saturday nights for the tight knit culture club to go to various rooms or cottages and drink and play poker for the night! Perhaps even get rowdy, who knew? That world was about to change.

With less than half the room still seated we enjoyed the hired entertainment. It was a very average country western group singing many known favourites as we traipsed on the dance floor hooting it up to the line dances (at least most of the women did!)

As I listened to the group, the "Audacious Annie" side of me appeared and spoke to me:

"Man you could do so much better than this! You could probably get a group of younger leaders from NYPA (the North York Principals' Association) to perform and sound better than these professionals! I bet you could get your friend and former teaching

Go Vibrant!

partner, Bruce, to work with you, get your creative juices together and produce a brilliant show! For sure ma'am!" I listened!

Yessir. I was audaciously ready to change the culture of the Gentlemen's Club. All I needed was a good plan. And for that I needed support!

Bruce and I had been the dynamic duo of teaching partners in two open plan schools, and had personally scripted and produced many musical school plays and other creative projects for staff and students alike. We were quite the team…like Regis and Kelly, like Goldie and Kurt, like Harry and Sally, you get the idea! The kids in our classrooms still to this day remember the magical amazing academic learning they did, among an atmosphere steeped in the arts and a culture of loving to learn. Such good days!

I filled Bruce in on what he had missed and my determination to make next year's conference better. Me, the rookie! The audacity! He thought I was crazy but went along for what he thought most likely was an imaginary ride. But once we started, he was in it all the way! We envisioned 50s/60s songs, 50s outfits and rewritten lyrics to popular hits that would match the plight of administrators in our schools. Our North York Board of Education was known as CHAMPIONS in Education. We would call our group '*The Champions*'. Ingenious!

We gathered together some newly appointed vice principal/principal colleagues who were contemporary friends as crazy and audacious as us. The originals were Maureen Capotosto, Neil Williamson, Anna Miyata, Johanne Messner, Bruce and myself. Excitement was in the air! We met at people's houses and my cottage to get this idea off the ground. Our meetings were filled with laughter, giggles and many ideas we weren't brave enough to put forth…yet!

The script was so clever, albeit a touch sassy, cheeky, in fact irreverent! A bevy of fractured knock-off songs to familiar fifties/sixties songs were written to add to the clever narration to move it along. We chose our "costumes". We prepared a number of very silly slides to go along with the songs we would sing. This was a trademark of Bruce and mine. One example of this was a slide of the 'Munsters' simultaneously shown as we roasted the trustees "Down in The Boardroom" to the tune of *Under the Boardwalk*. The theme, A Look at the Realities Of Leadership spurred us on to create songs like:

- "Let it Be Me" for the shortlist process (*Let it Be Me*)
- "Who put the R in the RDI DI? about a lengthy arduous process called Review, Develop, Implement (*Who Put the Bop in the B-a-bop-a-bop?*)
- "Look at that caveman go" recognizing the dinosaur administrators (*Alley Oop!*)
- "He's kinda tall, he's really fine…" a song about our Education Director (*The Boy from New York (North York) City*)

And many many more.

We took it to the Principals' Conference Committee and Johanne and I were put in charge of the entertainment!

Maureen became our stage manager who would run the slides on cue. The rest of us were willing to try to do our best at 3-part harmony but we needed another male. And one that could really sing. We recruited vice principal John McCullough, a giant teddy bear, kind and huggable with a strong, resonant, harsh deep bass voice and he could sing like no one's business. And he could read music! As I write this, I dedicate this story to him. He lost his life, in his early years as an administrator, one summer in South Africa during a mission trip. Sadly, his van hit a wild buffalo. We missed our gentle bass baritone.

Go Vibrant!

At one meeting, pompously pleased with ourselves at what we created, two serious questions arose: #1. Who would do the narration? #2. How do we possibly get the old boys "gentlemen's club" to stay and watch? The latter was the biggie. We had a brain wave! We would get one of the old boys to be our narrator!

We immediately set out to create a list of seasoned popular administrators who might fit the bill. We needed someone whom everyone else in the room would stay to watch! We listed them in order of preference and starting at number one we would make our way down the list.

Our popular choice was the well-liked principal for whom Bruce and I used to work a few years before and with whom we had developed a mutual respect and a friendly rapport. David Moscoe was more than delighted to join us, in fact, flattered, especially when he saw and heard us perform in my basement. "WOW! Just WOW," he said with awe! "I am honoured to work with you" That was David! Now we needed a name! We all agreed on Flash DeSoto. Perfect.

The birth of Flash de Soto and the Champions took place right there in my basement.

At one point we had second thoughts and I decided to take it to Superintendent Marguerite Jackson for her advice. She asked me first if I would do it for the queen? I responded with no doubts: "Yes I would!" She smiled, looked it over and told me with twinkly eyes that she couldn't wait to see the reactions! It was a go! At her retirement as Director of Education, many years later, we sang a song to the tune of Love Potion No. 9 with the line for that part, "But would you do it for the Queen?"

The dress theme for Saturday night at the first conference in which we would be performing as Flash DeSoto and the Champions was fittingly "Welcome to the Fifties", and many of our colleagues dressed up as if they had just walked off the set of *Grease* or *Happy Days*. Amazing what people will do for a "contest". We were nervous. Very nervous! Luckily our predictions that David's presence would assure that everyone would stay for the entertainment, came true. The current Director of Education was there dressed in jeans, a cardigan and slicked back hair. We were even more nervous. After our first faulty start, audaciously, I addressed the mic with…"OK starting again." Laughter followed. Then the many eyes watching us in anticipation, offering their support.

Flash de Soto: script in hand

"Hi Folks! I'm Flash de Soto and these are the Champions. We are a group of oldies stuck in a time warp of the fifties and sixties and we are here to entertain you…"

We heard the audience laughing throughout the whole presentation, especially that Munsters slide. We were like school kids in our excitement over our success, getting great pleasure from the accolades we received. It was the beginning of many more performances. It was the beginning for David to affectionately be called Flash for a long time!

You can imagine how ecstatic we were to receive a note the next week, from the Director of Education, North York Board of Education, Karl Kinzinger, extolling our virtues!

This says it all!

Dear Flash de Soto and the Champions
What a thrill it was to watch your group take over a whole evening of entertainment for the North York Principals' Association. You dared to be irreverent in a fun loving look at our administrators. Congratulations. Your group has single-handedly changed the face of the North York Board forever!
With deep respect,
Karl

We went on to be known throughout the whole school board and were requested for many more conferences and retirements, including the directors' and for each one of our members (except John). Each time we did so, musical director Bruce would declare "This is our last one!" We lasted until the retirement of our youngest chickadee Johanne!

I thank the audacious me of the 1980s

Audacious Me as a 64-year-old entrepreneur

It was only because I wanted her autograph that I allowed my friend to convince me, in March 2010, to attend her presentation. My sweet friend Amanda wanted to take me unwillingly to an event in which I was uninterested. At 64 I was knee-deep in a number of projects, busy with grandchildren, theatre productions and running a huge conference and more! However, when I found out that a woman by the name of Camilla Scott Eves was being honoured for achieving a certain level with this company called Arbonne International, I quickly changed my mind. Camilla is a famous Canadian actor, who

I have been following for years. I was a huge fan of her talk show and every play, including her leads in *Mamma Mia* and *Crazy For You*. The only reason I went to the fancy hotel for this "celebration" was to get Camilla Scott's autographs on the playbills I brought to the event. Oh yes, and I heard there would be free wine and food! Boom!

I might as well have arrived with a huge hat with glowing lights flashing "Camilla Fan Club" as I sat myself in the centre front row! What I was not expecting was to be so struck with the positive energy of participants, all passionate people, alive with enthusiasm and curiosity. Whatever they were drinking, I wanted some. I loved the vibe!

Back track…previous to that evening, I had endured 5 very painful surgeries to remove a melanoma stage 4 tumour on my right cheek. Pleased with the results (but not the scar) and although not at all a product junkie, I suddenly took to looking desperately for safer non-toxic products to use both inside and out! Hello!

They say stress is a big factor with cancer diagnosis. I was purposely on a journey to eliminate stress. I had already gotten rid of 150 pounds of stress by getting a divorce from him! Now I was looking to be around purpose-driven, bright, forward-moving people and do away with the stress feeders in my life. I was on a mission to purge friends who were too high maintenance, negative or Debbie Downers and replace them with positive go-getters. At the same time, I was researching how to eliminate toxins from my inner and outer personal care! Who knew I would find both in this very room.

I was watching via the eyes of a retired school principal, spearheading a charity for disenfranchised youth to see themselves as powerful leaders. As I listened to information about the company mission, the idea of entrepreneurship, helping others live a healthier lifestyle or introducing people to a new side career, caused a lightbulb to go off. I saw a whole new realm of the possibilities of me owning my own business and continuing to help others, this time anyone over 18, in even more and exciting different ways.

I forgot all about the beautiful Camilla Scott Eves, put my playbills back in my purse, and turned to Amanda and said "WE ARE DOING THIS! We have nothing to lose!" An audacious move? You bet! But then…why not? We seriously had nothing to lose and I was on the road to action once again!

The rest is history! Because of Arbonne, my skin glows, my healthy body shows up, I get to hang around incredible (and mostly younger people) from whom I learn daily. I was able to help my eldest son live his dream of opening a very successful restaurant in Toronto and I am present for my 13 grandchildren who see that life doesn't stop after 70!

Camilla Eves along with her fabulous sponsor, the incredible singer-songwriter Amy Sky, became my mentors and friends. I love the culture I work within. Have you ever wanted more? A chance to be your own boss? Build your own business? Bring out your audacity? Contact me!

I thank my senior audacity!

Back to that "comfort" coat. I appeal to you once again to unzip it a little at a time, step out and do something AUDACIOUS! Surprise yourself. It will increase your VIBRANT Vibration!

Create ABUNDANCE

As your life becomes richer in meaning and you have the basics you need to live, being vibrant in your life creates for you an abundance of much more than just material possessions. Vibrant living attracts an abundance of an appreciation of life, joy and strength of mind, body and soul.

I am blessed to have an abundance of experiences! Boy do I have an abundance of those, along with the abundance of smile/worry lines for the times I've laughed or cried! I am proud of each and every one!

I have an abundance of journals that remind me of the memories both happy and sad, of those times I spent doing and being, meeting and greeting, loving and living, with an abundance of problems to solve which has made me stronger and more joyful about what now surrounds me.

Add those abundant times to the abundance of serving others and now more importantly, but only most recently, serving myself and growing and learning every day to continue to strive to be the best I can be for ME first! Self-love brings you a VIBRANCE to flow with an abundance of love for others.

I attract abundance and wonderful things.

What a wonderful word ABUNDANCE, a word ending in the word "dance". Imagine the unique personal creative dance of your life, moving in and among negative feelings, dissatisfaction, emptiness, leaving them behind for the light and love that can be found elsewhere.

My dance with abundance

I started ballet and tap when I was very young (age 4 to 6) and only continued when my parents could again afford it at 9 years old. Times were tough. At age 10 I travelled by bus with another girl from my street, two afternoons a week after school. Thirty minutes away lay a very posh Ballet Studio run by an older Prima Ballerina from Russia. I have no idea how my parents afforded it! We must have had a friendly benefactor.

I was a quick study, mostly because I practiced by myself at home and gave free concerts! Mom and dad both saw me as having great potential, especially, a year later when I graduated on to point, and was given a solo from *Swan Lake* as part of the studio's concert for those of us under twelve.

I feared our teacher with a deep respect and worked hard to do my best each lesson. She was super strict! Imagine my shock, after a few years, when my mother was brought in for a parent conference and told that I was maturing too fast; my breasts were apparently "explodink", (the word she used) and she would need to strap me in with a special cloth, to keep me flat chested. Despite my tears and tantrums, my mother took me out of that school! My "flat as a pancake" lovely friend remained! I was devastated. I didn't speak to my mom for at least one dinner time.

Dance was my life. I lived to dance. I loved to dance. My family didn't have much money but they made the best of everything. They had tried sending me to a piano class, not private lessons. We did not have nor could we afford a piano. I had a cardboard keyboard on which to practice my lessons. Wonder why that did not work out!

I felt abundance and joy through dance. Dance covered up the shame or hurt of being bullied, of not being like the others, of being of a different religion, of having immigrated, of being poor and much more. I had to dance. It brought me happiness and joy! It brought me an abundant mindset so that I could look gratefully and appreciatively at what I did have in life! Dance took me to a world where I could believe I was deserving and worthy as I believed were others.

Five : Ace the As

Now what?

One of my "aunties" told my mom to check out "Jazz Dancing", where girls apparently could have big breasts. I stopped looking back, commiserating with myself at what I had lost with ballet, and started thinking of the alternative. *The Pajama Game* was a favourite of mine and I loved the dance numbers. New excitement for me! New visions!

Soon thereafter we moved to North York and my mom found a studio. Tap and jazz dancing shoes took over my toe shoes and I was once more in my element, this time experimenting with much more creative, freer unconventional moves, my favourite being swing! I'm grateful to my Russian ballet dancer for the classical skills I learned but also for kicking me out to find a much better suitor! During head cheerleading days in University and creating/teaching choreography for later Cabaret shows, I imagined myself as the female Bob Fosse!

Train your brain to see the abundance and not the scarcity!

I can make anything and change anything new with just a start!

Look in the mirror. You are magic. It starts with you. What you see in others is right there in you! We live what we visualize, what we ask for. Where we are now isn't where we have to stay. We get to go even further. You are in the driver's seat of your life, your love, your wealth, your business. Create abundance with an abundant mindset! Reflect inward. Uncover what is truly in you. Be abundant in showing up for yourself!

I believe in my abundant reality because I get to create it

HEY VIBRANT YOU! IT'S YOUR TURN
Claim Your Abundance

Make a list about those things in which you are abundant! I believe it will be longer than you think!

_____
_____
_____
_____
_____
_____
_____
_____

Live Life with an ATTITUDE of Gratitude

Making Attitude your friend

Make an attitude of gratitude your mission

Having a **positive** attitude surely leads one to love and live VIBRANTLY!

However, an attitude of **gratitude** is for me the ultimate! It completes the picture.

Five : Ace the As

> "Gratitude is the best attitude. There is not a more pleasing exercise of the mind than gratitude. It is accompanied with such an inward satisfaction that the duty is sufficiently rewarded by the performance"
> - Joseph Addison (late 1600s)

> "La gratitude est la mémoire si le coeur" (Gratitude is the memory of the heart)
> - Jean Baptiste Massieum (early 1800s)

> "Gratitude unlocks in me, the true purpose of my life, then, now and in the time left for me to be.
> To be grateful for those people and events in my life that fulfill my happiness and those who sponsor my life's journey, is what my heart has chosen."
> - Vivian Shapiro (Dec 1996 Gratitude Journal)

I try to start each day with a grateful heart, writing in a special gratitude book for good thoughts and thanks. For people or events that are not on my "appreciation" list, I now do what a friend suggested. I draw a heart and inside it, I write their name or in one word, the junk that happened and let it go. I wish them well and release! Such a tremendous power to be in control. Your good thoughts will rattle you down to the core of your soul so you feel it deep in your bones.

Planting the seeds of gratitude family style

Oh how those eyes rolled! It was my first Thanksgiving at his cottage with the new blended side of the family: Rowland's mom, daughter and son were there along with Marla, my friend. I was nervous. I was anxious. It wasn't easy trying to be a quiet low-key me! I worried about "being too much," especially around his mom!

At the dinner table, with a slightly trembling voice, I bravely suggested we do a tradition of mine, in which we go around the table and each declare what it is we are thankful for. Nevermind his mom,

Go Vibrant!

I was introducing this to his offspring both over 18, so you can imagine how well this went over! However, despite the looks they passed on to each other, they all agreed. I knew they were just humouring the new lady on the block.

Their answers ranged from humour to sarcasm to serious thoughts. Of course I recorded these in my journal. How much fun it is to read these now. I am thrilled to say that this became a family tradition, such that even the grandchildren engage in the tradition and have even added various ideas to these "Moments of Gratitude".

One such idea was to choose a person on the table and go around as each of us declared how grateful we were to have them in our life and why. Each one of us would feel so affirmed.

The responses often surprised the "chosen" to the point of both laughter and tears. Unforgettable moments. I believe they actually all still look forward to these "Family Gratitude Shares".

I smile at the poem found in my journal that first Thanksgiving with my new family, Oct. 1998:

I WISHED IT TO BE

Where did the summer go?
Here we are already giving thanks in October
for all that is and will be for us as we wish it to be.
An extended blended family are we
sitting around hors d'oeuvres of paté, red pepper dip, Jarlsberg cheese,
toasted pita and crackers sipping on our drinks of choice.
The spicy Bloody Caesar warms my insides and starts a buzz around my head.

Five : Ace the As

We are a mix of people whose lives are suddenly intertwined
and here we are celebrating Canadian Thanksgiving.
The aroma of roast turkey awakens the senses.
Rowland, his mom Helen James aka "Grammy James",
daughter Sarah and son Chris sit around the table with me
and my invited friend Marla
recounting favourite jokes, some a bit risqué
that Grammy James particularly enjoys.
Thank goodness for laughter!
We chit chat about many various topics that bring us smiles
or deeper discussions.
The golden maple leaves glimmer with the rays of the setting sun
which sparkle through the western windows.
The shadows of the pine trees dance in the wind.
Yes it's Thanksgiving.
A question is posed, a tradition being started, by the "teacher"
in the crowd
And you know who that is! Yup me!
"Let's all go around and say what we are thankful for!" she
suggests
"Where can I start?" says Sarah…"friends!"
"Family" exclaim Chris and Marla in unison
Helen announces, "Sarah has a Grammy who loves her!"
"Surrogate daughters"! "Surrogate mothers"! The list increases!
"Queen's University", "Dad paying tuition"
"Together moments", "a new wide spread extended family"
"Not being alone", "being loved"
"Children", "girlfriends", "mothers"

"Being up at the cottage with the family"

"Being up at the cottage with the new members of our family"

"The sun setting"

"Having paté on the table"

"My health", "feeling young and alive", "things we take for granted"

"My boyfriend" says Sarah now marking papers

"Chris' coke"…(the drink)

"Being able to think about being thankful"

"Being able to appreciate art, nature, love , food"

"Having Stussy as our pet"

"Smiling, feeling high, & watching life"

"Being able to make my own gin and tonics"

"Everyone being healthy"

"I don't have a sore bone in my body!" exclaims Grammy James

"Noone's dying at the present time that we know of" from the dry wit of Chris.

"What a horrible thing to say!" declares Sarah as she marks her 28th essay.

"Emotions". "Getting in touch with family". The list gets longer.

"Everything around me, even the mosquitos" says Rowl

"Easy for you to say," I counter, "You don't get bitten like I do!"

"Life!" "Yes to life!" We all agree, raising our glasses.

We are all thankful for living a good life together!

And later…at the firepit, the six of us silently gaze into the enticing flames

as if in a trance, broken suddenly by a shout:

"Let's sing campfire songs" (this time not my idea!)

And not seconds later the sounds of Chapin (not Chopin)

songs from Harry Chapin, Cat Stevens & Belafonte are heard.

(which surprises me coming from 20 year olds!)

The melodic voices of Sarah and Chris lead us

as they carry out their tunes with merriment trying to outdo one another

and I attempt to sing along but cannot believe they know all the words!

Singing, laughing, warming up,

A melodic warm and sensitive end to a perfect day

of Gratitude.

Their Dad must be so proud.

I miss not having my kids here. (someday I hope)

but I am grateful for these new moments in which I find myself!

Vivian Shapiro - October 1998

Gratitude is…   **G**iving
                    Receiving
                    Affirming
                    Thinking
                    Inspiring
                    Talking
                    Understanding
                    Dreaming
                    Expressing

HEY VIBRANT YOU! IT'S YOUR TURN.
Bring on Your A Game!

Write 3 things you are grateful for now (this very moment) …

1. _____
2. _____
3. _____

Over the next 5 days, continue doing this first thing in the morning and last thing at night, without fail. Each time you write, FEEL it. Really FEEL the gratitude flow up through your heart and soul and then…see what happens. Witness how it shifts your energy, impacts your day and brings on vibrant you!

I am grateful for:
DAY 1 MORNING

1. _____
2. _____
3. _____

DAY 1 EVENING

1. _____
2. _____
3. _____

DAY 2 MORNING

1. _____
2. _____
3. _____

DAY 2 EVENING

1. _____
2. _____
3. _____

DAY 3 MORNING

1. _____
2. _____
3. _____

DAY 3 EVENING

1. _____
2. _____
3. _____

DAY 4 MORNING

1. _____
2. _____
3. _____

DAY 4 EVENING

1. _____
2. _____
3. _____

DAY 5 MORNING

1. _____
2. _____
3. _____

GO VIBRANT!

DAY 5 EVENING

1. _____
2. _____
3. _____

If you weren't already doing this before and have filled out your 5 days of writing gratitudes, BRAVO!

I invite you now to buy yourself a special book for you to continue your practice of daily gratitudes!

THE A AFFIRMATIONS PAGE

Repeat those that you wish to apply to you today. Say it out loud!

I take ACTION to keep myself vibrant.
I take ACTION to service others.
My ACTIONS lead me to beautiful opportunities and ADVENTURES.

I ACHIEVE to the best of my ability to elevate my growth mindset.
I am an ACHIEVER.
I ACCOMPLISH my goals because I believe to ACHIEVE is the greatest force.

I live AUDACIOUSLY knowing I can take risks to reach my dreams.

I attract ABUNDANCE and wonderful things.
I believe in my ABUNDANT reality because I get to create it.

I have a positive ATTITUDE toward me, people and the work I am meant to do.

I choose an ATTITUDE of gratitude, thankful for the blessings in my life.

*"Three things in human life are important.
The first is to be kind.
The second is to be kind.
And the third is to be kind."*
- Henry James

CHAPTER 7
Six: Start with the N Game in Mind

Vibrancy sparks from Nurturing, Nourishing, learning to say "No", finding your Nirvana, being Naughty, but Nice and a bit Nuts

Here we are at Chapter N. I would like to dedicate the N page to think of completing your vibrant approach to life by focusing first on ways to:

Nurture yourself and others

Nourish your mind

Say No when you need to do so

Find Nirvana

NURTURE Yourself and NOURISH Yourself

Nurture or Nourish? I think these words are pretty interchangeable, but I have made them ever so slightly distinct to make sense of what they mean to me.

I see **nurturing** myself as nursing, tending to, caring for. When I nurture myself, I put myself first, honour myself and my feelings, love myself deeply and care for myself, my health, my wellness with consideration for my present and future being. This is no easy task! And I'm not particularly good at it. Being the empath that I am, I fight a losing battle with putting others' needs in front of mine. At the same time, I am aware of what I would like to do and I keep working at it.

I see ***nourishing*** myself as providing my mind and body with outside resources to help myself grow to be the best I can be in all aspects of life. I especially relate this to my mind and mindset. In order to provide and furnish my mind with the proper nutrients it needs to blossom, I purposefully focus on filling myself with growth opportunities, with love, with healthy thoughts.

I am so fortunate, as are we all, to have an abundance of inspiring and life altering books to absorb written by such brilliant authors as Tony Robbins, Mark Victor Hansen, Jeff Hendersen, Sarah Prout, John Maxwell, Gary Vanerchuk, Amanda Lang, Napoleon Hill, Susan Jeffers, Rachel Hollis, Michael A. Singer, Dr. Jill Kahn, Michael O'Brien, Matthew McGonaughey, James Clear, Jen Sincero, Paula Anstett, Mel Robbins, Hal Elrod, Katie Carey and the co authors of Entangled No More and all the other delicious sources that I have all around my office, bedroom and all over the condo not presently in view!

I am grateful for the many presenters, TED talks, retreats, and inspirational messages available to me that keep my cup overflowing with understanding to become strong and purposeful. I am fortunate to have found such beautiful individuals who have taken me through yoga, meditation, reiki, NIA, cardio salsa, dance, spiritual healing, body fitness and health experiences. I am able to focus on nourishing myself to continue to build healthy relationships not only with my tribe, but with all others, with nature, with my mind, body and soul in alignment to achieve a higher state of consciousness.

Six: Start with the N Game in Mind

I am much better at the nourishing aspect. I visualize the "feeding" of my mind to build a beautiful garden of love, the flowers of which I will bundle up not just for me but to pay forward to others.

Self Nourishing and Nurturing are part of the secret to feeling good about yourself to allow joy and happiness to flow through your bones. You realize you actually deserve it! One hard aspect that most of us have to do in the process is to learn to say "No", not only when people ask us to do things, but also knowing what to say NO to when travelling through life, and what to allow yourself to say YES to, on that long winding sometimes confusing journey.

Learn to Say NO

THE PLEAS TO PLEASE

I see the potential for
Magic, love and goodness
In everything.
I can tune into
Another person's needs
Before they themselves can.

I am a pleaser;
I love to love.
But sometimes I have given
When I should have insisted
On receiving.

And when I broke with tradition,
Cared for me
And expected more,
I was selfish, a bitch,
Or so I was called.

179

I would apologize
Instead of waiting for the apology
That should have been given to me.

How much of myself I gave away.
I neglected myself.
I need to listen to the pleas of my own heart,
The pleas to please, to please me!
Time to start doing for me
Without feeling guilt.

Vivian Shapiro - Jan 13 1996

Saying NO is something I have learned only recently. I used to say yes too easily to please others. I feared saying no in case I would then be rejected or hurt someone's feelings. I realize now that saying NO is an empowering way of living by my values, being transparent about my feelings and needs, and can lead to healthier, more honest relationships. It helps me feel empowered and free. The trick is to do so by balancing kindness and grace for others while holding on to your own self-worth. As well, learn to say NO to people, habits or aspects of your life that you know should be discarded to stay alive and vibrant. Here is a time I did not say NO:

Regrets I have a few…

And as Frank Sinatra sings in Paul Anka's very famous hit song *My Way:* "but then again, too few to mention". I encourage you to allow your vulnerability to break through during any deep self-reflection meditations, to allow some of your regrets to surface and be released!

One regret I have that still haunts me happened as a result of letting myself get stressed out and allowing myself to be negatively

Six: Start with the N Game in Mind

influenced by a naysayer in my life, and to this day I wish I could take it all back. It was a time I was afraid to stand up and say "NO!" It was a good lesson for me but it still hurts in the recesses of my heart when I remember my self serving actions.

My parents had stayed long enough! Their friends from out of town, especially bigger than life Freddy from New Jersey, were eating us out of all the food meant for the guests. My husband charged over to me, demanding that I ask them to leave so that we would have enough food for those who were on the "who's who invited list!"

I was a messed up, stressed out case trying my best to look calm, cool and collected. The bar mitzvah religious ceremony for my youngest son Todd was over. The Richmond Hill Club luncheon was perfectly awesome. The highlight for our guests and Todd, was the surprise musical skit depicting a "Typically Todd" week, performed by Bruce and me along with some of my friends and Todd's. The hours spent writing it, prepping the scenes and rehearsing it secretly were well worth the results. It was a huge hit! Now it was one down and two to go.

My months of planning and organizing were exhausting but I knew my expectations, though high, would be met with success. That night there was a dance party for Todd and all his friends in our decorated finished basement while our close friends and neighbours were lingering, nibbling and socializing on the main floor. The next day would be followed by a yummy brunch hosted in our back yard for all the out-of-towners and close family. I was managing well and keeping it all together despite the many months of bringing everything as close to perfection as I could.

My mom called me an hour before the evening function to tell me she and her friends were going to have dinner at a very nearby restaurant and asked if they could drop by for a bit and join the party and see their grandchildren Jody and Todd. Of course I was more than happy to oblige. My husband on the other hand was not as thrilled about this interference. After all, he sternly reminded me, "They will be attending Sunday's brunch! Why do they need to be here tonight?"

My own personal stress was compounded by the influence of my distraught husband's words to me once they were there. It gave way to the thoughtless side of me. Full blame here. I had a choice! Instead, I stormed over to my mother reacting to the message. With no gentleness whatsoever I questioned her as to why they were still there, reminding her that they had already eaten and why was Freddy devouring all our mini apps and desserts meant for those invited? OUCH! She looked shocked, but with poise and grace, as only my mom could do, she strolled over to my father and the next thing I know, they went downstairs to say goodbye to the kids and left without a word. As my dad was closing the door, he looked up at me and I saw the haunting hurt in his eyes. I had made them feel like second class citizens. I had treated them with such disrespect. I had not given my parents the deserved honour and joy of being proud grandparents. I felt and still do, even now, absolutely terrible.

The next morning, my dad, who was never good at doing the difficult emotional tasks, was assigned to be the one to call me to let me know my mother did not want to attend the family and out-of-towners' brunch gathering in my garden. No apology I could give, nor anything I could do or say at that point would change her mind. I cannot remember how I finally reversed her decision but it is quite possible I may have had Todd call his poppa John and grandma!

In any case, mom and dad did attend, along with the rest of the out-of-towners and our family members. It turned out to be a beautiful closing event. By the end of the afternoon, my mother, distant and silent at first, was back to being her lively self, and Freddy, with his entertaining personality, kept us all laughing, gay and merry! Even my boys enjoyed the adult company despite the fact that their friends were playing in the court in front.

I kept wondering why I had to be so cruel. It was a weak moment. My mom, at 66, would have loved to have partied with the kids downstairs for a dance or two. My dad was enjoying the part about showing off his daughter's inherited decorating and entertaining skills to his friends while schmoozing with our adult friends. I literally kicked them out putting my neighbours, none of whom I still see, first! I cut them off at the knees! Because I could not say "No. I will not do that!"

And the unfortunate thing? My dad passed on less than eight months later!

The other lesson? As an emotional creature, I am quick to cry and get hurt easily. When any of our adult kids do or say something I think is disrespectful or thoughtless without understanding how damaging it can be to us, their loving parents, I remind myself of that stressed out, anxious forty-one-year-old and how she reacted so dishonorably that evening. I loved my parents dearly, but I did not have the skills to deal with a little teeny problem that I could have easily just let go of. I could have said "No" to my then husband. I know they did not feel any love from me that night. It was not my intention to hurt but I was being selfish and inconsiderate. The lesson learned here for me is to try to understand what my adult children are dealing with and realize it has nothing to do with their love and respect for their parents! And with understanding, it too will pass. Love is stronger than mini hurting moments.

HEY VIBRANT YOU! IT'S YOUR TURN.
Unlock the Power of "NO"

What do you know you need to say NO to? What do you know needs to be replaced with a YES for something more positive?
Example: I say NO to: eating sweets. I say YES to: eating more vegetables.
What will you say NO to? How can you replace it with a YES to?

I SAY NO TO_____	I SAY YES TO:_____
I SAY NO TO_____	I SAY YES TO:_____
I SAY NO TO_____	I SAY YES TO:_____
I SAY NO TO_____	I SAY YES TO:_____
I SAY NO TO_____	I SAY YES TO:_____
I SAY NO TO_____	I SAY YES TO:_____
I SAY NO TO_____	I SAY YES TO:_____

**Now who do you need to gain courage to say NO to?
About what?**

_____
_____
_____
_____
_____
_____

Six: Start with the N Game in Mind

Someone said this to me once and I wish I could remember who it was or where I read it, but it stuck with me and every time I have enough bravado to say NO to something I am reminded of these words:

"I'm learning to love the sound of my feet walking away from things not meant for me"

Be one with NATURE

Cottage life has been a part of my being from as far back as I can remember. I thank my dad and mom for their love of nature, adventure and willingness to explore Ontario's beautiful northern landscape. I know that finding various summer cabins to rent always took a big dip in their savings for a house. In addition, I thank their very close European friends who were wise enough to buy land on a lake and generous enough to share with our family their early one-room self-built cottages, divided by curtains, complete with stinky outhouses.

I learned at a very early age that being one with nature was healing. Country life surrounded by nature, family and friends was refreshing, revitalizing and such fun! I learned a lot about life during the summer months spent either at rentals or with my mother's friends and children, who I always thought were our real life aunts, uncles and cousins until I found out they were not. It made no difference! The lake replaced the ocean for me. I learned to fish, row a boat, run a small motor boat, canoe, swim and dive off rocks at a very early age. I learned to water ski, first standing on a handmade wide wooden board (the original wakeboard) until I graduated to two skis and then eventually slalom. I took in the thrill of it all, except the mosquitos!

COTTAGE PESTS

I'd give away my chocolate
I'd never eat fajitas
If someone would remove from here
The spiders and mosquitoes

Vivian Shapiro June 2004

Following suit as a new family

I was one with the land, the water and nature surrounding me. Cottage life was my happy place then and continues to be so. In 1979 my then-husband and I bought a gorgeous sandy beachfront virgin piece of land in Lake of Bays, which until our divorce, was my retreat, my safe haven, my time for family, away from the busy city heartbeat. It was beyond a doubt one of our smartest decisions! Our cedar-planked building slowly grew over the years from a mockup Viceroy model on stilts to a beautiful four-bedroom, two-bathroom cottage, with a basement and all the amenities. It gave us hours of pleasure both with family, friends and also for me alone in silent retrospection. There is nothing like early mornings, sitting at the end of a dock, the quietude and stillness of the undisturbed misty lake before me. The chatter and cacophony of life all around, the plaintive call of the loon in the distance, the seagulls, the muskrats, the heron and more, set the stage for me to relax, breathe, read, paint, create poetry, write a journal, and rest in my own world, for the moment!

The hardest part of my divorce was saying goodbye to this labour of love but I felt good knowing my sons would still have access to it for years to come.

Six: Start with the N Game in Mind

A second chance

BACK AGAIN IN NATURE'S CARESS
(an excerpt)

*Drifting into old memories
I hear two lurking loquacious loons
calling to break the silence
and pierce the air with their haunting wails and hoots.
I reminisce of other such days by a similar lake.
How lucky am I to be able to continue to dwell
in northern cottage surroundings once more
where my soul can rest and drink in
the magic of nature and the repose it brings.
How lucky am I to have a stirring in me
that moves with the ripples of the lake.*

Vivian Shapiro - June 1998

I was fortunate with my second life partner to find one who shared that passion for cottage life and I gratefully accepted the invitation to share it with him and his family at their beautiful escape from the city on an island in the Kawarthas, where indeed I had spent much of my childhood! Such great memories! I was once again in my element, spending my early mornings breathing in the sights and sounds of nature at its best. And experiencing family life by the lake.

A little anecdote here comes to mind as I explore another **N** word: **Naked!** And what better thing to do but **Go Naked in Nature!**

"What if someone sees you?" shrieked the voice from the bedroom, astonished by my "naked ways". It was in our early days together and he was not used to seeing me so comfortably prancing around the cottage and deck just being me! There is nothing more freeing than being able to strut around in one's birthday suit whenever the opportunity lends itself. I believe in going naked both physically and mindfully, but for now let's release those inner inhibitions. Free yourself! Start physically!

Being on an island, far enough away from the three other cottages inhabiting the eight or so acres, gave me great allowance and privilege to really be free to be me during my early morning alone time (when there were no family or guests visiting). I especially loved going down to the dock wrapped only in a very large colourful beach towel, disposing of it slowly and slipping into the cool, milky texture of the, as of yet, undisturbed lake. I was responsible for the first ripple to circulate! And I would ask myself as I quietly stretched my hands and legs out in breaststroke style, preparing for my laps, "What good can I ripple in the world today?"

"But what if someone sees you?" repeated Rowl as I returned for breakfast.

"Who would see me?" I queried. "The cottages are too far away, the boats travel on the other side of the lake, and I make too many splashes for the fishermen to want to be here", and so on. "Well, what if people are like me and like to watch what's happening across the lake with binoculars?" the questions continued.

"Well then it's their lucky day isn't it!!" I replied.

No more questions asked.

Not everyone is as fortunate as I to be a cottage owner and the great thing here is that you do not have to own one to be one with nature. Whenever, however you can, drop the cell phone, get off social media, get out there, observe, be one with nature and if you can, go naked!!

Six: Start with the N Game in Mind

Find your NIRVANA

What is your Nirvana?

Finding Nirvana in the spiritual Buddhist or Hindu traditions goes very deep and takes serious forms of practice to get to the ultimate goal. I apologize to anyone who may be offended for my taking great liberty here with the word Nirvana, for my own purposes simply to find my own personal vibrant journey of a joy I can gift others. I should probably call it NIRVIVA!

Nirviva as my nirvana

For me it's my place of perfect peace, my place of happiness, my state of enlightenment, my own manual for my life where I can open my own book at any page and find my true self. This is always a work in progress. It's a journey with many curves and takes various directions, sometimes surprising even the best of my intentions. I'm OK with that. I'm human.

I notice in my life two types of people in the world: those who choose to be vibrant and live with positivity, joy and vitality, and those who choose to be apathetic, dull, and negative. Of course there are varying degrees of each category. For me you either lean one way or the other.

Truth bomb: joy and happiness doesn't come from fame, fortune, or material possessions! Happiness comes from within. Happy people choose to make themselves happy by creating joy in their life and living vibrantly!

I created my own *Manual of Healthy Habits for Living a Vibrant Life,* born from many different intimate discussions with like minded searchers along with what I gathered (even with my shortened retention) from the many books I have devoured. Add to that, what one learns from life experiences, and what I discovered from my own journals. I have put together what I try to do to reach my **Nirviva!** It's a steady work in progress.

For purposes of this book, I will render the list into practices instead of affirmations for this chapter. Please feel free to repeat these as you read them.

To find my own place of Nirvana or *"Nirviva"*, I present to you

My Magic 20

1. **I practice meditation.**
    a. *Silence your mind to find inner peace.*
    b. *Inhale for healthy and happy.*
    c. *Exhale to let go of emotional stress and tension.*
2. **I practice loving kindness.** (*Metta*)
    a. *Being kind and treating people with love, dignity, and respect makes you happier ... TRUE!*
    b. *Every time you perform a selfless act, your brain produces serotonin, a hormone that eases tension and lifts your spirits.*

Six: Start with the N Game in Mind

3. I affirm and uplift others.
    a. Happiness is directly related to the happiness of other people.
    b. Showing compassion promotes happiness for all.
    c. Give someone a hug. Let people know you are grateful for them and appreciate them. Provide a listening ear if needed.
    d. Act with love and acceptance, accept people who deserve respect.
    e. Respect all living things.
4. I see setbacks as set ups rather than treating problems as drawbacks.
5. I focus on positive thoughts.
    a. Rid your mind of negative feelings to release deadly toxins in your body that give way to depression, anxiety, and stress.
    b. Focus on the good things in life.
6. I develop an attitude that aligns with my belief system.
    a. Be authentic and be the true you!
7. I dare to dream big.
8. I savour the present.
    a. Stop and smell the roses.
    b. The present is a gift!
9. I practice mindfulness: a contemplation of body, feelings, state of mind.
    a. Your actions flow out of what is in your heart and your mind.

Go Vibrant!

10. I am an early riser with a ritual for a successful day.
    a. Create a circadian rhythm that helps increase productivity, and puts you in a calm and centered state.
11. I keep a gratitude journal.
    a. Express gratitude for what you already have.
    b. "The happiest people don't have the best of everything; they just make the best of everything they have."
12. I focus on what I can control and how to make it better.
    a. Don't sweat the small stuff. (This is especially hard for me!)
    b. Life's not always fair. Accept it!
    c. Life is also too darn short. Make changes not excuses.
    d. Benjamin Franklin once said, "He that is good for making excuses is seldom good for anything else."
13. I surround myself with forward thinking, optimistic people with positive energy.
    a. Treasure those who will encourage you.
    b. Dump the naysayers.
    c. Surround yourself with people rooting for your rise!
14. I take and make time for my partner, family, and friends.
15. I follow what's in my heart.
    a. What people say about you is none of your business!
16. I try to talk less; listen more.
    a. Listening keeps your mind open to others' wisdoms and outlooks on the world.
    b. The more intensely you listen, the quieter your mind gets, and the more content you feel.

Six: Start with the N Game in Mind

    c. This is not easy for me so I stay conscious of my talkativeness and try to change to be a listener.

17. I develop healthy habits for my body and mind

    a. Everything you eat directly affects your body's ability to produce hormones, which will dictate your moods, energy, and mental focus.

    b. Studies have shown that exercise boosts your self-esteem and gives you a higher sense of self.

18. I find ways to volunteer to help others.

19. I surround myself with love.

20. I live a vibrant life.

Be NAUGHTY but NICE and a Tad NUTS

An unlikely match

Can you imagine how you might feel? You are 28 years old. You were super excited to get away from the cold weather and the dysfunctional relationship you have finally left. You have arrived at your destination, in beautiful warm Mexico. This Club Med is one of the best recommended all-inclusives, known for its gourmet food and great-looking single men and good times. You eagerly look out the steam-fogged window of the rickety old bus transporting you from the airport. Since you are going single, you have been matched with another single person, one you do not know, and you cannot wait to meet her.

Your roommate arrived on the earlier bus and she stands there with your name on a sign, eagerly awaiting her new friend. Her hair looks sort of ashy? Blond? No, ashy! And she's old! Like for sure in her late 40's! Great! She is probably going to want to go to bed early and not want to party and for sure think old thoughts. Disappointingly, you emanate the best smile you can and you saunter over to her, already presuming you will not have a good time.

The above story was not mine! I was the old 49-year-old! The 28 year old was Marla. I sensed a little hesitation when she approached me. To be honest she looked more like 18! That did not phase me one bit because as broken as I was, just fresh out of my separation, I was naughty and nuts and ready to make this trip fun and frolicky. I was ready to do it with whomever would like to participate with me! Marla had no idea what she was in for.

I think she started to get the idea that she had lucked out when I explained to her why our room was so much more luxurious, in one of the better, more accessible locations of the resort, than the others. Our original room was accessible by about 300 steep steps! And so small. I did my usual naughty but nice thing of treating the concierge with authentic kindness first. I widened my smile, brightened up my eyes, as I then explained that I had a few sciatica and heart problems (true) and if there could be something lower, I would be most grateful. He was immediately ready to help and after conferring with the manager, they whisked me off to a spectacular large room with an amazing view and much fewer steps. Apparently it was for the assistant head G.O. (Gentil Organiseur) of the "Spirit Team" of that resort, who was unable to come. Club Meds were one of the originators of the premium all-inclusive clubs, hosted by G.O.s (Gracious Organizers for those speaking English) that kept you entertained morning until night. As we wound our way to our room, many already greeted me by name. I think I won sweet Marla over then!

If I didn't do it with that little ace up my sleeve, we won each over naturally. As she unpacked, I lay on the bed and we chatted to get to know one another better. Within 20 minutes we felt a huge bond of kindred spirit-ship. We had similar experiences with controlling men and we were both in the same place of confusion, anger, fear, needing time for ourselves to boost our ego and believe in ourselves once again! And that's how it all started!

We were naughty, nice and nuts on the trip! We played hard, laughed hard, drank hard, smoked up hard, and a few more things not necessary to mention. We hooked up with another Torontonian, Alan, and we became the Three Merry Musketeers of Three decades… late 20s, late 30s, late 40s. We had a blast! We all got lost in the reverie of this Peter Pan Neverland in Mexico, forgot our troubles and got happy. We bonded, became good friends and supported each other. We healed in the narcissism of it all!

The next year Marla and I booked a cruise together and continued our shenanigans, such as getting ourselves moved to a better dinner table where of course we noticed a father and his three sons sitting. These guys looked like they had just leaped out of a Chippendale Calendar! We spent the entire week cajoling around the islands with our new found friends, platonic fun for me, a romantic happening for Marla.

CRUISIN'

Tis true a cruise
Can heal a bruise
Something to choose
Drink lots of booze
Make no excuse
Take comfortable shoes
Act like a flooze
All on a cruise

Vivian Shapiro - Dec 31 1995

Twenty-seven years later, Marla and I are still super friends. For Marla and me it was meant to be. At the time, Marla's mom had early stages of Alzheimers in her mid-50s, and I became a sort of older sister/surrogate mother to her. I did not have daughters or daughter-in-laws at that time so it filled a great need in me as well. Somehow a mom, suddenly alone, who needs a companion for a show, a play or a weekend in wine country, does not usually get that role occupied by sons. Marla and I became part of our own mutual admiration society. My journals are filled with Marla/Viv stories, many of them naughty, many of them nice and for sure many of them nuts. I could write a book alone on our adventures that span every emotion possible. And maybe I will.

At 55 and 76, we still get naughty together. Now Marla is going through a divorce and I am able to empathize completely as the old feelings can easily be stirred up. I feel blessed to have her in my life and am grateful I am able to offer consolation and advice when needed. We cry together, or for each other, hug each other as much as we can, share our personal stories and find many times to laugh together. Most of all we still carry on allowing naughtiness in our life.

We all need someone willing to get crazy, go nuts, do naughty. It's what fills our soul with fun-loving vibrancy. Call it diabolical, mischievous, impish, playful, frisky, devilish, or silly shenanigans. Whatever it is, do it! And find someone to do it with you!

THE N AFFIRMATIONS PAGE

Repeat those that you wish to apply to you today. Say it out loud.

I NURTURE myself by feeding my mind and soul knowing:
I have so much love in my life.
I am so loved.
I give love and receive love.
I deserve love and affection.
I love and accept myself.
I love the person I am now and the person I am becoming.

I NOURISH myself by knowing:
I have grit and I don't quit.
I build habits that help me be successful.
I am vulnerable and open to change.
I allow myself to be challenged by zipping out of my comfort zone.

I say NO to those things that do not serve me and yes to what I know I need.
I am comfortable saying NO when I need to look after me.

I find my NIRVANA by being centered, balanced and at peace.
My NIRVANA is my being light and love.
I allow myself to be where I am to be in my personal "NIRVIVA".

I enjoy my life allowing myself to be NAUGHTY yet NICE.

Being "NUTS" with crazy energy keeps me laughing.

CHAPTER 8
⭐ Seven: Fits You to a T

Get Vibrant through Tenacity, your Tribe, your Team, Togetherness, the True you, Tenderness and Thankfulness.

Try out your TENACITY

Tenacity in life can definitely help you keep up a vibrant, sprightly, high-spirited life. I love to check dictionaries for words such as this, as often they are misunderstood!

tenacity (n.)
early 15c., tenacite, "quality of holding firmly," from Old French ténacité (14c.) and directly from Latin tenacitas "an act of holding fast," from tenax (genitive tenacis) "holding fast, gripping, clingy; firm, steadfast," from tenere "to hold," from PIE root *ten- "to stretch."
[Online Etymology Dictionary]

tenacity noun
the quality of not giving up something easily; the quality of being determined
[Oxford Learner's Dictionaries]

If someone calls you tenacious, you're probably the kind of person who never gives up and never stops trying; someone who does whatever is required to accomplish a goal or to get through hurdles or challenges, never allowing yourself to be discouraged and moving on and forward. Often by family members you may be seen as being stubborn, as I am sure my family has viewed me and still does! In reality, you are a go-getter, unstoppably vibrant!

Only in reading my journals about my thoughts of determination and moving forward when challenges came my way, do I now realize that I, in fact, lived with a tenacity of which I was not even aware.

Get rid of that annoying mark!

In September 2004, I had this very annoying mark in the middle of my right cheek and sought a plastic surgeon. Two skin doctors had agreed this was simply a cyst and that, for the cost of $350, it could be taken off in a simple 10 minute procedure at the hospital. With just a small bandage on my cheek, we headed to our cottage to enjoy the Labour Day holiday weekend. Easy Peasy.

I did not give it another thought until the phone call with the message from Dr. Samuel, left during our Jewish holy days of Rosh Hashanah, caused my worry lines to dig in. "Please call my office and make an appointment. I have something to discuss with you." I repeated it several times to see if the tone could give me an indication of the seriousness. The seven days leading up to the scheduled appointment were worrisome sleepless nights. However, I convinced myself that he just wanted to sell me on some costly anti-aging facial procedures like Botox, chin surgery or whatever it is they do at these clinics now besides serious surgery.

With Rowland away in Prince Edward Island, my sons were the first to hear me say, heavy with tears, that I had to have immediate surgery for a growing tumor, a case of melanoma, on my face. Dr.

Samuel actually thanked me for my vanity as he hoped we caught the tumor early. He and Dr. Lenneck were both so sure it was just a benign cyst. Somewhat apologetically, he explained to me with drawings what he would be doing to my face. Not a pretty sight. I could expect scar tissue forming, throbbing, and a big scar down the middle of my cheek. The good news? My $350 for what was to be "cosmetic surgery" was returned thanks to our health care system.

As scared as I was with the "bordering on Level 4 Melanoma" Clark Level III diagnosis, my tenacious spirit already informed me that I was going to get through this with flying colours! "You got this Viv," I wrote in my 2004 journal and I prepared myself for the surgery ahead. I did write a page of all my fears and next to it a list of affirmations assuring that I would conquer this, in the days when I didn't even know what affirmations were!

Rowland got the news long-distance and he and my family all sent me flowers. I felt loved and cared for. But I was terrified.

October 8 2004, my good friend Amanda's 27th birthday, was also "The Chunk of the Cheek Cut Day" as I named it. Dr. Samuel's usual nondescript serious bedside manner always came apart with me because I could always get him to smile or even laugh. I believed with all my heart that my results would be positive and I would just have to face the battle scars, knowing I would always have a story to tell. I remained steadfast in my belief that "this too shall pass" and that it would not deter me from anything I was still on this earth left to do.

I felt I had to cheer up my many supporters who sent well wishes the day before and thus, after the surgery, I sent off a mass email to help them feel better! Yup…that's me…

October 9 2004

Dear friends and family,

"Just as the sun is breaking through the clouds here in cottage country on our Thanksgiving weekend, putting an end to the early morning dismal gray, so too are my spirits breaking through. The black clouds have passed and I am feeling good. I am feeling positive that all has been removed and that my scar, in time and with a hell of a lot of good makeup, will seem trivial and insignificant in the scheme of things. I slept well even though I had to avoid sleeping on the "snoreless side". I think Rowland was extremely worried about a sleepless night for him (not me), due to my snoring. Apparently I did not! The magic of pain meds!

What's it like? It's one hell of a long cut with over 50 plus stitches. OMG! Oh well what's one more wrinkle?...8 to 10 days until I get results…Am anticipating being a conversation piece for a while…Thank you for your support. Happy Thanksgiving and reflect on all those things in life for which you are truly thankful. I know I have many blessings, among them you!"

I share with you all a little poem I wrote to keep myself in good spirits!

AFTER THE CUT

The deed is done
The cut? Yikes it's long
The stitches are many
But the pain? It's not strong!
In fact, it is scary
'Twas tight and 'twas taut

Seven: Fits You to a T

But now the pain
Simply is not!
"This is a good thing!"
Martha Stewart would say
Too bad she's in jail
For her crimes she must pay
But me, I am happy
Though my scar will be yuk
People may stare
I dont give a f%$#k
I'm sure Samuels got it
Feeling healthy and well
And though it ain't pretty
And I look like sheer hell
Little 5 year old Jack said
As he looked with a pout
At my bandaids and strips
What'd you do? Oh! Wipe out?
Yah Jack, that I did
But I'm getting better
Gonna move on with speed
Cuz I'm a go-getter!

Vivian Shapiro - Oct. 2004

November 3 2004 was my third, more extensive surgery to remove more, as the margins were not clear. The result of the surgery was depressing because all I could think of was that I will no longer be Rowland's "Goldie Hawn"! I truly looked like something from a freak show - lopsided, one eye drooped down, lip curled up. I felt like my skin was stretched over canvas.

While one cannot always find humour during rough times, I try. I found this story in one of my mass emails to my supporters. It even makes me smile now!

November 4, 2004
Hello again friends,

I share with you this surgery story so that you will know that although they are removing tumours and skin and the like, they have not removed my sense of humour. At least, not yet! I will write this from the first person narrative as if you are reliving my experience! Here we go:

Needles are being punctured in my cheek. My eyes are closed but I hear Dr. Samuels as he comments rather loudly, "Now just look how funny her lip looks after I have injected the local". I ask who he is talking to? He tells me it's "Take a Grade 9 Kid to Work Day"! Great. I open my eyes. I am introduced to Chris and Elizabeth. Elizabeth looks like she is going to faint, so I quickly shut my eyes again. Within a few minutes, Dr S. starts working on me. Luckily I am numb and frozen from chin to eye. I hear a gurgling sound and a whoosh of someone leaving the room. I look up to see Elizabeth gone. Chris lasts through what seems to me to be a heck of a lot of cutting! After I am made to look like a mummy covered in sterio strips, Chris, in the honesty of youth, chirps, "Miss, I hope you will be OK. I just want to tell you how lucky you are (pause), that you, um that you, well that you could not see what happened!" Thank you Chris! TOO MUCH INFORMATION! However, I later gave him a Future Aces Smiley, from a notepad I had, to give to kids for positive reinforcement. He got one for his bravery. Elizabeth was nowhere in sight.

Despite this set back, I wouldn't miss my Cabaret rehearsal retreat. I continued all my Future Aces presentations including the 6 day conference. The school kids loved it when I told them I wiped out on roller blades! Thank you little Jack for that idea! Just a little white lie!

Unfortunately I was not quite finished with the cutting.

Nov. 18 2004 Journal entry: The results are in!

Whoops. Melanocytic cells are still approaching the margin. Back to the cutting board. I feel like a steak that still needs more fat taken off. (If only!) My birthday is coming up in two days and is not going to be as happy as expected.

Nov. 26 2004 Journal entry: Cut #4.

"A cut above the rest," I hope. People are now really starting to take me seriously and the best thing is that I am learning how loved I am by family and friends. These are the times when you have to work really hard to rid yourself of painful worrisome thoughts and engage in as many positive ones as possible. I am having a very hard time.

With tenacity, I took the physical pain, doubt and depression, and flipped it around with declarations of faith because I was determined to see this through and come out the right end! Determined! I had much more of life to live and I had yet a legacy to leave this world.

On a pink paper, written with a fancy fountain pen (oh yes, I had a penchant for good writing pens!), I wrote in my best calligraphy:

I will survive!
I will be OK!
I will still be beautiful! (even if it may only be from the inside)
I have amazing friends and family!
I have a supportive loving partner!
I am loved!
I am supported.
I will be well and healthy!
Now let's do it and let's get it done!

I stuck it on my mirror.

Go Vibrant!

The December verdict

> Dec 8 2004
> I could barely breathe waiting for Dr. S to get on the phone
> DR. S: Hello.
> ME: Yes hello Dr. Samuel.
> DR. S: Would you like me to read the report?
> ME: *(thinking: No, I thought we would just talk about the weather!)* Sure.

The only thing I heard was "the area at 9 o'clock is 1.1 mm clear of the tumor with no cells approaching the margin"... The rest was a blur.

> ME: This is good?
> DR. S: Yes.
> ME: *(big audible sigh)*

I was then sent to Sunnybrook and then in the new year 2005, to the Toronto Network Hospitals where I was now under Dr. Lipka's care. She felt it would be necessary to go in one more time. My bff Sharon W. was there to shelter me from my disappointment. This time I would be going fully under, for an overnight stay, and they would remove sentinel lymph nodes to ensure the cancer cells had not travelled. That would be surgery Number 5! I had regular visits with the doctor before and after the surgery. What was very sad is that a young gentleman patient, with whom I conversed on many of my visits, did not make it. I was fortunate! My lymph system had not been attacked. The only thing that could have been attacked was my ability to brave the journey. I did not let this setback define me.

Yes I have had more skin care challenges and have received more removals of other pre-cancer dangerous cells, but the main thing is the main thing.

Of the several doctors I saw during this journey, they were all impressed with my steadfast hold on my faith to heal, my sense of humour, my determination to see this through without stopping my life, and my positive energy. One of my doctors asked me to speak to a couple of his patients to tell them of my experience. In my 4-week visit after Mohs surgery on my nose to remove the aggressive squamous cell carcinoma, he had to look at his charts to believe that I only had the surgery 4 weeks prior. He could not believe how fast it healed! I believe, important to any healing process of the body or of the mind or the heart, you must deal with the present reality by believing in your future. The past is gone. You cannot do anything about it anymore. You have the present, your gift, to take the action you need to grab in order to have the future you want. Tenaciously, grab the bull by the horns and ride it till you get the better of it! I was proud of myself, that despite the scars and the battle, I was able to come forth strong and better for the experience! Tenacity! Be tenacious! Even better:

Be TENACIOUS + Be AUDACIOUS = Become a TRAILBLAZER!

Get Your Vibe from your TRIBE

In today's world you often hear people saying "I found my tribe" to mean they have found the people with whom they feel comfortable; like-minded people with whom they wish to work, play or hang! Then there is also the tribe that chose you, like your parents and the familial structure built around your family. This would also include your spouse and their family.

Experiences you had growing up, including your relationships with your grandparents, parents and siblings, can affect your joie de vivre, as you enter the different stages of growing up. Upon reading my journals' words about my family members, I can clearly see the positive aspects I inherited from each of my bloodline. I seem to have been fortunate to have taken the best of all those close to me. Genetics or choice? As hard as I was in being judgemental and critical of my elders, I see now that I was truly fortunate to have had good role models.

Did I do that intentionally? I do not know. I would like to think that some of my behaviour patterns were as a result of the awareness I had even at a young age, about what would be most valuable for me. That's not to say that I did not get some (or even lots) of the less desirable traits set before me, but I know I focused more on the admirable character traits to absorb.

Your inherited tribe is your tribe. Love them for what gifts they can bring you even though they may be hidden. Too often we allow ourselves to blame our upbringing and our parents for some of our undesirable traits of which we are not proud. When we blame our adult behaviours on what we perceive are as a result of the hurt from inherited loved ones: spouses, parents, relatives, siblings etc., we make excuses for why we are unhappily the way we are. And then we have an excuse to stay the way we are. I was lucky to be loved even though I did not always feel that way. Find the gifts your tribe gave you and are still giving you to be the person you turned out and are turning out to be. You have choices. If there was pain, turn it into power…the power of YOU! Your tribe can fuel your vibe! I thank my

Seven: Fits You to a T

upbringing and even painful moments for the vibrance I was able to gather to be me!

In 1992 I personally saw a therapist to figure out my role in the dysfunction of my marriage which was hanging on by a thread. In reality it should have ended long before its duration of 28 years but I was being…tenacious! The doctor gave me homework and asked me to write about my father, something to share with him next session.

And this is what I wrote in my 1992 journal. I took it upon myself to write an essay for the doctor. The sections in italics are my actual entries.

A gentler man you could not find

Dad:
Gentle, sensitive, thoughtful, kind, unconditional, pleaser, selfless, passive when needed, creative, artistic, sharp dresser, giving, absent minded, procrastinator, lover of life, traveller, soft, well loved, proud of family accomplishments, worrywart, sensitive, loyal, trusting, empathetic, talented.

A gentler man you could not find.

Selfless and completely adoring of my mother.

He worshipped the ground she walked on and secretly, I think, he never felt he was good enough or deserving of her.

He was artistic and had a real flair for anything to do with design.

My dad and I had a wonderful relationship. Though he was extremely overprotective of me, always fearing my involvement in high risk sports or activities, he was a tremendously loving, caring, hugging, gentle father.

Spanking was quite normal in those days of child rearing. When my mom, who wore the pants in our house, gave my dad the order to discipline me, she expected him to deliver a "good smack on the bum". He never could! He would give me a light tap…more like a feather but

209

asked me to cry out or yell loudly so that my mother would think he did his duty. How I loved him for that.

He took great pride in watching my artistic ability shine. He read with pride my homemade cards and poetry and I know he felt a kindredship in our mutual love of art.

I loved watching him in his role of display manager for a retail chain as he made signs, dressed the mannequins and created thematic window displays. When I worked one summer as his display assistant, he beamed as he announced to his team which window I had created!

My best times with him were from as soon as I could remember him until I was about twelve and then later as a married woman, until he passed on at age 71. Too young!

When I was little, I was his son as well as his daughter! I did everything he liked to do, even though in those days there were specific "boy things" versus "girl activities". I became proficient at handling tools and helped my dad, the builder, create my entire bedroom in our first little matchbox of a house! He taught me to paint rooms and houses, fish, row a boat or putt around in a motor boat as long as it was super safe! I even put my own worms on a hook and took my own fish off the hook.

My dad was a great story teller about both serious and amusing incidents and experiences as a young boy in Germany. On my visits to their mobile home in Florida, when my energetic mom was off playing tennis early in the day, my dad and I spent a lazy morning together as I listened to his childhood stories. I truly wished I had taped them.

Dad and I shared two weaknesses in common: procrastination and absent-mindedness. I still have those traits.

Physically I will always remember my dad, in his best days, slim, young-looking, slicked-back shiny black hair, gallant in appearance, with a large toothy smile. I inherited that smile that people often comment on in pictures: "Ah there's that Leinung smile!" I'm proud of it! As

Seven: Fits You to a T

a teenager I looked a lot like my dad, but in my adult years, more of my mom came through. My sister maintained his looks…tall, long legs, long arms, slim lanky look, olive skin that I've always envied! And to me, my oldest son is a clone.

My dad always had a slightly slouched over walk. He was slightly over 6' tall, taller than all his European friends, with a very fast clip in his walk that both my sister and my son have inherited! I always had to run to keep up with him and now have to do so with them!

When I turned 13 or somewhere around then, I changed and it affected my dad. I became strong-willed, mouthy, bratty, determined, argumentative, embarrassed about my parents' German accents, and independent. In other words, I became a teenager! Did I mention my sister was 5 ½ when I was 13, so sweet, so cute and so good as gold! That fact might have contributed to my "rebel" era, along with my jumping hormones.

The worst thing I ever said to my mom and dad (and there were many awful words that exploded from my lips) was in the form of an order I gave them when a few new friends from high school were coming over one afternoon after school. I was so embarrassed at their accents (even though they spoke excellent English, especially my mom) that I told them not to talk at all when my friends were over other than to say hello, and then to disappear in their bedroom or something! Ugh! How cruel! How I wish I could take that back now! The look on my dad's face? I can still see it!

When my sons were little, I believe I was the strictest mom on the block. I was also the only working mom who left her kids with nannies during the day, something that didn't go over that well with the stay at home moms until later when they envied me for my freedom and career! (But that's another story.) When I would set down my guidelines with my kids, different from their friends' rules about coming in for dinner, homework, TV times, end of play time, clean up, bedtime etc., I would hear them curse me as "the meanest mother on the court!" I basically disarmed them by answering "Thank you. I've been attending Parent School to achieve that! I will tell my teacher that I reached that status with flying colours! Do I get a certificate?" My dad didn't have those "come back" skills.

My father became very disappointed and frustrated with my rude behaviour and my mother became violent. Being so super sensitive, he took a back seat to my upbringing, and now mom ruled the roost more than ever. My mom and I were like oil and water. There was a painting of a tiger in our living room and I honestly thought it was my mother in her other lifetime. A reincarnation for sure!

This adolescent, so insecure about herself, striving for recognition and independence, saw the insignificant passive role her father was now playing in the family and hated it! I saw it as a weakness. I think this stemmed from my frustration of knowing that my dad was possibly the only one who understood and cared genuinely for the "unique" me I was. Now he was not even standing up for me, even though sometimes I know he empathized with me. I actually pitied him. What did I know?

I often said to my mom "I will never ever marry a man like dad". I saw him as a wimp and I certainly didn't want to marry anyone like that. Little did I know how that would come back to haunt me. I most certainly did not end up marrying a man like him and, once I realized what a gem he was, I wished I had! I had better luck the second time around!

Seven: Fits You to a T

My best, yet saddest memory of my dad was in January 1987, when he flew in from Florida to check his congenital heart failure with his heart specialist in Toronto. My mom stayed in Florida as it was a big expense to fly. He stayed with both me and my family, and then with my sister and hers, for a week each. We spent many moments down memory lane together and I remember coming home from work each day at lunch to prepare for him a German style delicacy just like Mom did everyday… kartoffel (potato) soup, and aufschnitt (cold cuts) on rye bread as an example. My whole family made an effort to be home each night for dinner. It gave him great pleasure to see his grandsons growing up as lovely polite young men. He witnessed our family life being well taken care of with respectful conversations between husband and wife and children. He commented how well all four of us took on household responsibilities, given that we were now nanny free and both our careers were taking off. We put on a good show!

I heard him talking to my mom each night about his admiration for our family scene and he knew I would be all right. Our heartwarming conversations had an aura of sadness, as I could tell my dad knew his days were numbered and he would not be with us much longer. After all his tests were done and his medications lessened his bloated legs, he returned to my mom in Florida. Three weeks later on February 7, 1987, my dad died of a massive coronary. I miss him every day and I love that he visits me regularly in the form of a butterfly! (But that too is another story!)

> "I am not afraid of death. I am afraid of being an invalid, one whom you and your sister and your wonderful mother, would have to look after. I couldn't bear that."
> - John (Hans Joachim) Leinung - January 1987

After I finished reading all of the above essay in italics to my therapist, next session, he stated, "Well, you really gave that your all!

I have never had a client write so much. You should write a book!" (Interesting he should say that!) "As for the content, hmmm, that was not what I expected to hear."

We discussed a few more things that session and he then sent me home this time to write about my mom. He lightly suggested that the mother story would most likely give him the information he expected to hear.

Mom, the family matriarch

My mom? My therapist certainly heard a much different story. She was a whole different matter entirely and, in short, these traits were those listed to him about Ursula Ader Leinung:

Besides the fact that I thought she was the reincarnation of the ferocious tiger fiercely staring out from the painting on the wall, I saw her as:

Super strict

Domineering

Compulsive

Obsessive

Orderly

Sarcastic

Biting

Critical

Possessive about her possessions

Easily flustered by me growing up

Disciplining me through rage, hitting and yelling.

Seven: Fits You to a T

I told him stories such as:

One day, in her rage, she threw a heavy wooden cutting board at me. Luckily I had good reflexes and ducked in time for it to hit the big picture window behind me. (My dad was not impressed with the bill to fix the window.) I wondered what my little sister was thinking.

I was afraid of my mom, terrified in fact. I was afraid to do anything wrong, afraid to spill food on the table cloth (which I did all the time and still do!), afraid that I had not set the table properly, afraid I let the potatoes boil too long, afraid to use something that was hers, and the list goes on and on.

Even though I was a terribly insecure young girl, I remained a happy child. Fortunately I focused more on the absolutely wonderful vibrant things about my mom. There was something very appealing about Uschi! Yes, fortunately on the flip side, there were many fabulous characteristics she portrayed.

She was phenomenally beautiful and always dressed to kill (mostly from outfits chosen by my dad). To my friends, once I lifted my self-imposed "no talking when my friends are over" ban, she was charming and welcoming, always offering treats as was her traditional European custom. They all adored her! They were in awe of her beauty. They told me how lucky I was to have her as my mom. And I believed them. I tossed away the negative thoughts. After all, my friends must know best!

With her social friends, she was the belle of the ball and the hostess with the mostest, holding many dinner parties and lively events (decorated thematically with my dad's artistic touch).

She was a hard working mom for as long as she could be, played tennis skillfully till she was 90, and volunteered for many charitable organizations and hospitals. She was the strong, powerful matriarch of our family. She was a role model of vivacity.

Although she was extremely critical of me, and hard on me even as an adult, she did try to make me feel beautiful and talented, despite my own attempts at self-deprecation. It was a bit of a paradox. As I have mentioned, I will never forget her saying to me time and time again as she watched me attain various successes in life: "Vivichen, what can't you do!?" Well mom, I cannot manage a TV set with all the series of remotes and what to click first and second and so on. When alone and trying to get a program, I get so confused, I end up reading a book instead! Thank goodness now I just need to give my remote a verbal order!

My therapist's reaction to this account was, "OK that explains a lot. It helps me to better understand you now." I never was sure what he meant but, I will say, he opened my eyes up a great deal to my circumstances and the decisions I needed to make for myself.

Five years after my separation, in 1999, both my sister and I (individually) had the chance to accompany my mother to Leipzig, Germany when she was 79 years old. The German government was offering former Jewish residents who had been forced to flee Nazi Germany a free trip to Leipzig as retribution for the horrible crimes committed to them, their family and their community. I spent seven days with her and a few of her former childhood friends with whom she reunited after six decades.

We visited her childhood home, school, synagogue, parks and attractions, all now rebuilt after the war, in the city in which she spent a joyous, entitled 16 years, until the Gestapo forced her, her mom and dad to escape with nothing but a suitcase and money sewn in their clothes. Our nights, after our hosted excursions, were spent with me on my computer writing down her stories, some already heard but not recorded and ones new to me. I learned a lot that week about my mom and why she had to be so tough. I felt deep guilt for all the thoughts I used to have and for all those times I screamed "I hate you! I wish you were a real Canadian!"

I was so fortunate to have such special individuals for parents and I attribute various aspects of my own vibrancy to both of them. From my mom, I reaped over the years her vivaciousness, bold attitude, tenacity, courage, womanly power, orderliness, joie de vivre, social being, and general love of life. From my dad, I believe I inherited his artistic creativity, love of travel, ability to dream, and sense of humour, all adding to the formula for me to traverse my world with a vibrant sense of self, even when I did not wholly believe in myself.

If you were not as lucky as I was to have such endearing parents, look to those who were influential to your upbringing as positive role models and find out what characteristics they had that, through osmosis, became a part of you! Be grateful!

Stuff about siblings

"Siblings - the definition that comprises love, strife, competition and forever friends."
- Byron Pulsifer

If you are fortunate to have a sibling with whom you are close, this is indeed a blessing for you to create sibling vibrance!

In my case, as you know, I only have one sister and you already know that a seven and a half years' difference does not create the ideal situation for friendships and commonalities. I was out of the house at 17, married at 19, which leaves her as a 10 and then 12 year old, not even a teenager yet, to be living with my parents. We didn't know a lot about each other for years and suddenly she was the "only" child at home instead of me.

As adults we became closer but, even when she married and had children, they were each nine years younger than each of mine. She was into diapers and preschool and I was among teenagers that talked back! We did become closer when we suddenly and unexpectedly did have something very much in common! With her actually taking the lead a year before me, we both found ourselves divorced from our first husbands and in second relationships with all that entailed. I am truly fortunate to have my sister, Karen, in my life and am so pleased that we did not let age, cultural, career or personality differences, or family dynamics interfere with a basic sisterly love one can only share with someone who has the same family genes and history. I have found, in fact, that we have a lot more in common than we ever really could have imagined. Even though we may have different stories of our parents, seen from different perspectives and different eyes, I am thrilled to have someone with whom I can at least share these tidbits of hidden gems as we recall our parents' foibles, quirks, idiosyncrasies, endearing qualities and virtues. Often when together, especially in the kitchen or entertaining arena, we look at each other, notice what we are doing and realize what habits we BOTH have inherited from our hostess mom! The best part for me, these past years, is how we can laugh at ourselves, seeing how we are truly birds of a feather who, as the "Leinung" sisters, strong, fierce and sometimes harsh, like our mom who lived to 101, will surely stick together in all kinds of weather!

I am putting this out here as a special message to you, sis: Karen, I am sure with your organizational and care taking skills, you will be the one to look after me in my very very senior years while I write poems and sing to you. I might even kick up my heels and dance vibrantly!

Careful what you wish for

I always wished for a large family. There was always just my mom, dad, sister and me and, for a time, my Opi and Omi and a few relatives in Portugal. Most of my friends had so many cousins, aunts and uncles, and my family seemed so small in comparison. I loved spending Christmases with my highschool friend Janice and her large family who filled their festive house with such gaiety. Yes I always desperately wanted a large family. You would think that in that case I would have had many biological children. It was initially my intention. I found however that my desire to be a career woman overcame my desire to bear more children. My husband and I brought into this world two beautiful and adorable sons who filled my heart with such love and meaning, but I married an only child with a half sister, and so the family dynamics were still small scale.

Presently my family extends to my loving second partner, my kind younger sister and her second husband, my two biological adult children and my three other wonderful gifted children "by another mother." Rowland came into my life with a very large family dowry. Although he was an only child, his mom was one of six and thus Rowland had several aunts and cousins on his side and, via his ex-wife, three additional children and their close cousins! Although they may have all already been over 18 when I met them, I felt and still feel their love and their presence.

The members of my tribe have all been influences in my life and, through lessons learned via relationships with each of them and their wonderful partners and their many delightful children, I continually learn to live life as fully and as productively as I can as a vibrant sister, mother, step-mother, mother-in-law and grandmother. I hope beyond hope that I am understood and not just someone who is too much to handle! I know I can be that too! It comes with the territory. The sense of family, being together; the tears, the joys, the Christmases, Easters, Thanksgivings, Jewish celebrations, cottage times, vacations, and birthday events fill my cup. Family celebrations look exactly as I had envisioned them as a child. I am so happy I was not careful with my wishes! I am truly part of a very large family! And I LOVE it!

Try a little TENDERNESS

> *"There is an endearing tenderness in the love of a mother to a son that transcends all other affections of the heart."*
> \- Washington Irving

You may wonder how tenderness fits into living a vibrant life. Tenderness does not always come easy to me. I admit it. I carry out life in a big passionate way that tends towards loud, bordering on high expectations of myself and others including my children. As a forward thinking woman of my era who strove for success in all areas I touched, not only motherhood, I was hard on myself and hard on those within my immediate grasp.

Yes I was vibrant. Maybe overbearingly vibrant? I had to learn to tame the shrew with something that could balance its outrageous force. The yin to the yang. The Companion to Vibrance. The kindness to balance the severity. The answer: *Tenderness*. I am still, via my spiritual practices and readings, trying my best to harness this, as one uses tenderizer to make a steak more succulent and easy to cut. Tenderness leads to connection. I am awesome at affection and at expressing emotion. I am a touchy feely person. I have lots of kindness cells travelling throughout my body. Empathy and sympathy ooze forth easily. Tenderness? Not always. I am more like a tender tough broad. And today…a tender tough old broad!

Vibrance has a muscle to it, but our greatest strength comes not from these muscles but from the tenderness of the heart. Tenderness gives vibrancy its wellspring to the fountain of joy. I work daily to complete my habit of living life with that joie de VIVre, yet remembering tenderness.

Tender be my boys

It has always been, and continues to be with great tenderness inside, that I watch my two biological sons grow up, each so different in their personalities, with a tenderness for what they are and a deep respect for what they still will become. Just as this book has been, in somewhat of a joking fashion, dedicated to them, it's time that I acknowledged them in my stories.

With each one I have my own set of dynamics, love-ins, proud moments, frustrations, fights, tears, joyous moments, sufferings, hurt, my "feel-so-bad-for-you" times, laughter, questioning.

Jody is my first born, and in my tender eyes I still see him as a child who was: timid, cautious, wanting to be around mommy, quiet, respectful, very sweet, happy to play games, sporty but not highly athletic, a lover of songs, sensitive, helpful, hardworking, a follower of guidelines, a good student, friendly but shy. Then, skipping through his independent, uncommunicative teen era, as an adult I saw through my tender eyes how he grew out of his timidity and caution, became athletic in sports he liked, displayed a great deal of creativity, bought a motorcycle, and surprised me with his career choices, first in film and then in the food industry. I marvel at how he shows a great deal of respect to those he works for and alongside, and to those he manages, and how loyal and supportive he is to his loves. Jody won many awards for his talents, is hardworking, is valued as a colleague, strives for success, remains kind, is appreciative of others and takes time out for hobbies. I am so super proud of his many film and life accomplishments, including creating and opening an amazing, highly-recommended and talked-about foodie restaurant that, despite Covid challenges, he and his business partner Michael kept alive! Bravo for the risks you took, Jody, to bring your dreams to the fore. I love you so very very much and am blessed to have beautiful Kaori, Alejandro and Noriko in my life too!

Todd always remains my baby, and in my tender eyes I see him as a child who was highly imaginative, independent, full of life, very athletic, creative and artsy, a bit prone to tantrums, very affectionate, complimentary, one to stand up for the underdog and for what was fair and right, very bright (sometimes too bright), a good actor with a gift for words. Many of these traits still exist including being a huge visionary, a hard relentless worker, a problem solver and planner for the future. He admits he goes against the grain and makes noise. His professions of radio co-host, hosting his own radio station on Sirius, to becoming a serial entrepreneur and CEO of a company he started from scratch, give testimony to his tremendous ability to think fast on his feet. He is bigger than life to watch and listen to on social media and I am so proud of his many successes. Huge hugs to you Todd, for having a determined mindset and, as a visionary, for seeing past the present into future possibilities as a role model for your beautiful children. Todd, I love you and I thank you for keeping my family "large" with the stunning Irina, and Sawyer and Scarlette to love and adore.

Seven: Fits You to a T

Both now grown men with families, my sons, as do all sons, need to still know that they will only truly be grown men once they can understand and accept that, in their mother's eyes, they will never be fully grown. So, if you are reading this, Jody and Todd, just give up now and that will solve a lot of grown-up son frustrations! Mothers are strange creatures. Moms want their sons to be babies forever, such that they can give them advice. They want to continue to love in a nurturing way, yet carry on grown up conversations. Moms want to get excited about all the amazing things their children are still accomplishing in their lives. Get used to it!

Sons are a different breed. They have been my thrills, my heartthrobs and my terrors, yet I will always love them so very much. I started motherhood at the age of 25. Despite what I told them in jest, about attending "How to be the Best Mother" school, I only hope that through my attempts at being the best mother I knew how, I raised them to respect people, especially women, stand up for others, and most of all be kind. I hope this tender tough mom passed on to them my philosophy of not taking life too seriously and to find love, joy and laughter wherever and whenever possible!

Even in their late 40s and now early 50s, my sons still chastise me for being too much of an advice giver and not a listener. I am learning to release the abundance of words and problem solving skills I possess, ready to spring forth at any second. I release them to the silent air to make room to listen. I will learn to become a vibrant listener. It's not too late. We are always learning and growing. And most of all I will do as the famous Otis Redding sings: *"Try a little tenderness."*

The joy of blending

If our entire blended family were to be in a room, it would have to be an extremely large one. Along with Jody's and Todd's families, the vibe from my tribe also comes from the delightful mix of loving personalities and characters that I embrace as my own to cherish along with my own birth children. My tenderness goes out to the Dunning tribe for my gratitude to have you all present in my "large family" wish come true! Julie, Dan, Camryn, Reed, Lindsay, Anna, Chris, Carla, Georgia, Max, Joe, Isabelle, Sarah, Alex, Ella, Charlie and all the fur babies - I love and adore you! If I were to include all the Dunning stories, I would be into a second book!

What does all this have to do with vibrancy? Though the word vibrant tends to put an image in one's mind of being loud and boisterous, there can be vibrancy in tenderness and a deep love for your tribe. Look for those family moments that play those vibrant notes that keep your heart singing!

Be part of a TEAM

"None of us, including me, ever do great things. But we can all do small things, with great love, and together we can do something wonderful."
- Mother Teresa

Along with your inherited and biological tribe, are those you cultivate to be team players: your colleagues and your personal friends. Who are the people you are attracting? Are they like-minded in success? And are you a TEAM player?

Seven: Fits You to a T

Again I have been blessed to have had and to still have such awesome and amazing friends and coaches from whom I have gained so much. I hope I have, in turn, inspired and motivated others as they have me. For me, it was important to have positive, upbeat, motivated, fun loving, challenging, individuals in my circle, both to play with and to work alongside. I learned to look for those who could help propel me forward to live a better life and accelerate my own personal goals and growth, while I helped them with theirs. It was also important that they found value in our friendship, business relationships or connection as a mutual admiration society.

These individuals and groups did of course change over the course of time and during the evolving nature of my journey. Some have been with me for what seems to me to be a lifetime! It did mean that as I matured and recognized the negative influences surrounding me, I had to make decisions to let certain people go, not in a harsh way, but just simply gently removing them from my "most wanted and adored" list!

The people you spend the most time with shape you. They influence your attitudes, character and behaviours. The course of your life, what you say, think, do and become, can be influenced by those you hold in your circle. They are a tool for you to live the life you desire and deserve. If you wish to live vibrantly, then I invite you to invite VIBRANT people into your life. Find your dream team to be able to fulfill your own dreams and help them fulfill theirs. It's your choice!

"According to research by social psychologist, Dr. David McClelland of Harvard, [the people you habitually associate with] determine as much as 95 percent of your success or failure in life."
- Darren Hardy, The Compound Effect

A side bonus to working together with a brilliant team that creates magic and success, is the lifelong friendships that can develop. Such was the case with Amanda and me. You have heard me reference Amanda for Cabaret, Future Aces and Arbonne. What started off as one working relationship soon led to two working relationships and then three. At the same time we were developing a close personal friendship, surrounded by love and learning from each other.

We met when she was 25 and I was 56. Even though we are 31 years apart, have different learning styles, bicker like an old married couple and often have to work through battling creative versus logical processes, we work! We come up with solutions! Our teamwork makes dreamwork. It also created a crazy close camaraderie, enjoying together those many things we have in common. What a wonderful world it is when you can work hard and play hard with someone you find through a collegial start, with whom you then become forever friends. With "great love and together", we do create wonderful things and we do have wonderful times.

I am forever grateful for this beauty in my life to be able to freely enjoy things like:

- *Blue Jays games and yelling clever sayings to our favourite players*
- *Staying up very late binge watching Netflix series when on biz trips, laughing until it hurts*
- *Leaving our Future Aces team behind to hang out in a club in Barbados with the NHL hockey players and later joining Lou Gossett Jr. for poker at the resort in which we were holding our conference for young Bajans*
- *Joining the 2 day weekend to End Breast Cancer as part of Paula's Posse, dressing the part and overnighting in a tent*

- *Treasuring butterflies everywhere we go as messengers from our angels above, her grandfather and my father*
- *Skinny dipping many midnights in the lake*
- *Bingeing endlessly on snacks we know we shouldn't have but what the heck*
- *Creating a partnership blackjack scheme that works every year we are in Vegas*
- *Singing Boogie Woogie Bugle Boy in two part harmony everywhere we can, including reworking the words for special birthdays*
- *Taking many mulligans (shh!) while golfing and laughing it off*

And the list goes on and on and I know it will continue to do so! Amanda recently wrote to me:

"Our family and friends find it hard to understand our close friendship. They wonder why someone now in their 40s would be best friends with someone now in their 70s. But what is an age? You may think my youth has helped keep you young over the past 20 years. In reality, it's your vibrance that has made me feel younger!"

So true. Maybe it was me that started the crazy, but having someone who will work it with you, no matter the age difference, older or younger, keeps us all vibrant. Disappointing experiences with past friends or colleagues led me to search for a mix of people who would cover those characteristics I admire or value.

Take Laine. Although 20 years younger, her unbelievable work ethic, her sense of adventure, her admirable experiences living and working in many different countries (now a resident of Mexico!), her history of being an immigrant mother finding herself in Canada, single handedly bringing up her daughter, her sense of style and incredible knowledge of haute couture able to make others, me included, look beautifully put together, on a low budget, her spirituality and her sense of fun appeal to me. We have helped and encouraged each other in different ways that have helped each of us on our own personal journeys.

I would be remiss if I didn't mention my unique and talented friend Gail here, just to prove that I do make friends with people my age too! As colleagues in the Toronto Board of Education, we had a deep respect for each other's talents as creative educators. One year, as teachers in the same school, both teaching gifted students with whom you had to be highly imaginative, we shared ideas and became closer. It was solidified to become a lifelong friendship the day we both walked into the staff room on November 20 (my birthday)1981. My teaching partner (yes Bruce) was on the sofa strumming on his guitar and as I walked in, with Gail close behind me, he started playing and singing *'Happy Birthday'* with other staff members joining in. Before they could get to the line that would say *'Happy Birthday dear Vivian'*, Gail, with great glee and delight shrieked "Oh how did you know? How sweet of you to remember my birthday!" She then realized they were singing to me. We discovered we were twins by another mother, born exactly on the same day, same year, but in different countries. Since then, along with our common interests in spas, theatre, music, the arts, creative gifting, implementing programs for kids, decorating, planning events, cooking and much more, we continue to have fun discovering different ways to celebrate our mutual birthdays each year!

Of course there are many others from various walks of my life, for whom I am forever grateful. You know who you are and, whether you are from a past team or are part of the present team, I know I continue to profit from our experiences.

Seven: Fits You to a T

In the words of Glinda from Wicked, singing Stephen Schwartz's iconic song, *For Good*:

I've heard it said that people come into our lives for a reason
Bringing something we must learn
And we are led to those who help us most to grow, if we let them
And we help them in return
Well, I don't know if I believe that's true
But I know I'm who I am today, because I knew you.

Choose Togetherness

Aside from your Tribe and Team we all need those who provide a sense of togetherness, a community in which to enjoy our vibrant being, whether it be in a dance club, playing a sport, playing online games, the gym, artistic venues etc. Where best can you be your true self?

Love is such a powerful force. It's there for everyone to embrace -
that kind of unconditional love for all of humankind.
That is the kind of love that impels people to go into a community
and try to change conditions for others,
to take risks for what they believe in
-Corvette Scott King

Find vibrant communities that offer you light, laughter and liquidity! Find your togetherness opportunities in circles, in communities, that remove the dullness and help keep your vibrant self as polished as a new diamond.

Go Vibrant!

In my adoration for acronyms, I present you with yet another for "Community" and what it means to me.

Communities can provide the following:

C CONVERSATIONS in a COMFORTABLE safe place to CONNECT
O OPTIMISTIC OUTLOOKS in life with like-minded beings to leave behind negativity
M MEANINGFUL and MAGICAL MOMENTS that focus on fun-loving spirited activities
M MINDFULNESS that brings MOMENTUM to self and inspires you
U UNDERSTANDING of self through UNIFICATION of interests
N NURTURING to the mind, body and soul with NATURAL heartfelt conversations
I INTERESTS to share with new INDIVIDUALS
T TEAMWORK and a sense of TOGETHERNESS
Y YUMMINESS like a gourmet meal waiting for you to devour, as the real YOU

SEVEN: FITS YOU TO A T

HEY VIBRANT YOU! IT'S YOUR TURN.
Traits to Treasure

What positive traits do you possess?

_____   _____
_____   _____
_____   _____

What traits (behaviours, attitudes, philosophies) do you wish to **disallow** in your life.

_____   _____
_____   _____
_____   _____

What 6 traits do you most admire in others?

_____   _____
_____   _____
_____   _____

Make a list of the 10 people with whom you spend the most time.

_____   _____
_____   _____
_____   _____
_____   _____
_____   _____

Beside each one above mark an **A** if and only if you greatly **admire** them for the TRAITS they possess. Now look at the list.

Go Vibrant!

Are there some changes you should make to surround yourself with those who have the traits you most treasure? Your thoughts?

_____
_____
_____
_____
_____
_____

Before I end this chapter with my notes on what I thought would be my final T word, THANKFULNESS, I would like to say a word about forgiveness even though it does not fit into a chapter full of words with the letter T. By dubbing this Be TRUE to Forgiveness, it can hold its own in this chapter!

Be TRUE to Forgiveness

The pain of betrayal

Pain, anger and mistrust filled my body and soul. It is hard to describe the deep betrayal I felt from a very dear friend of mine, when I was just about to turn 50. A very deep distressing and painful betrayal. This was a friend I had met later in life when I was 40, but there was a synergy and love that grew between us almost immediately. For purposes of this book, I will refer to her simply as Her or She.

Seven: Fits You to a T

The frivolous fun four

With Her, for the first time in my life, I became part of a foursome of girlfriends whom I suddenly felt I knew all my life. We met at the Bayview and Sheppard YMCA and, what started as a Sunday morning class together, was soon followed by bagels for brunch and then, fairly soon thereafter, became greater than the "hole". (I hope you got that!)

Because I had moved so much as a child, I never had a solid group of friends that were a part of my lifetime journey. I had developed close friends on a single basis. I had a lovely set of university girlfriends all present at my wedding so long ago but, other than a few reunions, we drifted apart during our adult lives. This was different. I had a feeling this was forever!

I realized what it was like to finally be part of a group, a solid "get-together-all-the-time" kind of group that lived and breathed each other's lives. I loved and adored them all and was overjoyed to have each of their very unique and distinctive personalities bring more vibrancy to my own. We were a "Ya Ya Sisterhood" sort of clan.

There was "Crazy Raisy", whom I met at our respective sons' hockey game. She was pumped full of vinegar, had chutzpah like I'd never seen before, was an exercise fanatic, a wannabe singer (think Whitney Houston), managed a band and performed with me in Cabaret. We did the New York scene like no one else could. She brought out my Broadway best. There was Diane, whom you have met already, a volunteer fitness instructor at the Y, determined, competitive, very active with a solution ready for anything! Diane and I actually met at the Y when the two of us decided to write a letter to management about the poor quality of classes run by their volunteers (not Diane's classes of course!). And then there was Her. She was Diane's friend and brought to our group a great sense of fun and

Go Vibrant!

humor, a love of beer and wine, and a sense of fashion that we all admired, especially when we needed to borrow something from her overflowing closets (yes, more than one!). We all became besties, but most of all She was the one with whom I had a special relationship that I could not explain.

With Her, I am not sure why, there was an immediate magnetism that existed. Perhaps we had known each other in another lifetime. Perhaps we had been sisters. Who knows? We have even been told by others that we sort of looked alike.

As a group, we did everything together in the decade of my wild and wooly days from 40 to 49. We trusted each other with our stories, our vulnerabilities, our worries, our joys, our dreams. We traveled together, socialized as couples, spent time at my cottage both as couples and as single girls (the latter being the better time). We met at the YMCA (with some, each day), early in the morning, followed by a Y team morning breakfast before we all headed to work. There really wasn't anything we didn't do together. The best thing we did was laugh and giggle and dance and have fun! Especially when we were not around our men!

I started to forget my frugality much to the chagrin of my then-husband. With all my besties' influence, and especially Her's, I started taking better care of myself, treating myself to mani pedis and, with the introduction to Giancarlo, much needed loving hair treatment. I joined more fitness classes, and treated myself to a fur coat (sorry…it was the fad in those days) and more stylish outfits to match my new administrator role. She was one of the most generous people I knew, and often events I had to attend were done so in her outfits which were always right in style!

And then it happened. I was separated and alone on one of the most painful journeys of my life and She was no longer available for

SEVEN: FITS YOU TO A T

me for reasons that are not ones I wish to bring up. Suffice it to say that I was heartbroken, had many sleepless nights and, as I wrote about my pain in my journals, I found words I didn't even know existed to call her. Terrible words!

The most difficult thing for me was that, given that we shared mutual friends, I was put into situations of seeing Her often for special events, like kids' bar mitzvahs, baby showers, wedding showers, weddings (for one of my girlfriend's daughters AND for one of my girlfriend's) and other such events. In some cases we were placed at the same table! And while I wanted to hate Her so much, there was a part of me that missed her so much. Like magnets, we were drawn to each other to find time to chat, though awkward at first. In time, we could be found grooving together on the dance floor to "Celebrate Good Times" after our guys were done! I know…weird!

Hate, anger and pain can do damaging things to your psyche and your health. In the early stages of our disconnect, I wrote her a scathing 7 page letter, that in retrospect I should have ripped up. Yet I did not and it was sent. I guess it was so destructive that the next time we found ourselves at a function together, it was like she had bodyguards around her. When I went up to the buffet where she was in line, someone came and whisked her away back to the refuge of her table. I was the crazy lady and they weren't sure what I would do next. Interestingly, I read a copy of this letter recently and it really wasn't all that bad. It was more sad than bad.

The letter however is a result of what toxins can do to you. When you do not eject the tape that continues to play cruel scenarios over and over again in your head, you dull your senses. Toxic thoughts dwell like demons in your mind, executing any carefree cells and destroying the kind, understanding, compassionate minions of your mind. Hatred is toxic beyond measure.

It was soon thereafter that I came to my senses realizing that Harry Hate had me locked in a prison cell. To know me, you would know that normally I do not hold grudges, and my anger at anyone or anything is short lived. It is one of my endearing traits. In this case, yes She had more than deeply hurt me; but after seeing the fear and hurt (possibly even the guilt) in her eyes that day, I scared myself. Who had I become? I realized that forgiveness was something I could choose to do. I was ready to move on because the love I still felt for her in my heart was beating louder than my temporary hate.

To forgive is to set a prisoner free and discover that the prisoner was you.
- Lewis B. Smedes

Releasing the prisoner

I am not sure who did what first to bring us back. I suppose it started when, soon after the hate letter was sent and received, we were together at our mutual stylist's salon. She was with Giancarlo and I was with the colourist. Poor Giancarlo. Hairdressers of course always know the whole story and he had tried so hard to ensure we were never together on the same day and time. He was sweating. But there we were. I braved it and went up to Giancarlo's chair. Just a few simple words to relieve the tension. "Hi! Well I guess this was bound to happen sooner or later and here we are. How are you?" Whew! She seemed terribly uncomfortable, nonetheless she managed a smile with "Fine, hope you are well". Giancarlo tells me he was so so proud of me that day!

After that when our paths collided, we naturally had moments of being drawn together and the conversations became fun and easy. I still was not her friend per se, but we were friendly.

When disease or sickness comes your way, they say you can tell who your real friends are. In the year of my surgeries and scare with melanoma, She was there from day one asking me if she could visit me at home, if I felt it was appropriate. When cancer interfered drastically with her life a few years later, I had to up the ante. No matter what had occurred in our life, I knew with my heart of hearts that I had to be there for her to offer her love, support and care. Slowly, we resumed our friendship and now it's even stronger, more spiritual than ever.

People thought and still think I was and am crazy and cannot understand how we can be such good friends. Remember what I said in the last chapter…what people think of you is none of your business. She is a special person. We have a special friendship, maybe because of what we went through. I'm thrilled to have her in my life.

If you are in the throes of thoughts of retaliation, revenge, hate and anger, please know that you are poisoning your own mind and dulling your shine. Forgiveness is more of a gift for you, for your future, than it is for the forgiven. And, other than those non-negotiable times when your grief is due to life-threatening actions, if you can find love in your heart to add to the equation, then go forth and be bold with your choice to forgive. Try it, you'll like it!

You can't forgive without loving. And I don't mean sentimentality. I don't mean mush. I mean having enough courage to stand up and say, 'I forgive. I'm finished with it.'
- Maya Angelou

I have never been a fan of eradicating someone from my life entirely. It just does not sit well with my nature and who I am. Granted, I have not had someone do something to me that is personally physically harmful or life threatening. I have not experienced horrific abuse of my body or mind. I have not been tortured or sexually abused. Had this been the case, that person would be completely non grata in my life. I see no other direction here. I do not know how anyone can live with such trauma and forgive. That is another story all together.

I am talking more about being disrespected by someone in the family or by a friend such that you are truly deeply hurt in a way that causes a rift or disconnection. Time outs are always good solutions. Sometimes time allows us later to see the whole story. Sometimes time gives us a different perspective. Sometimes experience and age give us a different feeling from what our reactions were in the past.

Understand the art of forgiveness

I encourage you to understand what forgiveness can give you. I express my thoughts based on my own experiences with feelings of pain, anger, revenge and hate. Please know that I am a Scorpio… True to my sign, if you mess with a scorpion, you must watch out for its sting! And when you mess with me, the very same is true. On the other hand, I may not forget but I usually find the right moments for forgiveness. I really cannot see the sense of eliminating people entirely from my life. Whether it be for a few weeks, a few months or years, friendships may take a break. For relationships to be completely eradicated, it does not make sense to me at all. My vibrant life continues as a result of those in my life, even those who were banished who found their way back with a renewed vitality and respect.

I ask you at this moment to think of someone now whom you have shut out of your life. Even if it's someone with whom you have had a horrendous argument and who you have "punished" by not speaking to them for a week! Is the reason still so important? Are they still alive? (Nothing you can do if they are not!) Do you actually remember them with some fondness despite the "incident"? Do you have enough good memories to outweigh the bad?. What would be so terrible, if you reconnected? What would it take for you to make this courageous move?

And for those whom you simply cannot bring back into your life, release and let go.

Be true to yourself without keeping toxins running rampant in your body!

Be THANKFUL

I am so thankful that in my life I have found those who have challenged and inspired me, so much so that, at various times, I wanted to spend a lot of time with them. Find your people and it will change your life. No one is here today because they did it on their own!

For those of you who were or are on my organic MOST WANTED and ADORED list, you know who you are and I thank you to the moon and back for your advice, adventures, companionship, influence, inspiration, laughter, love and support. In this book's acknowledgement and gratitude section, I will be listing all of you who come to mind that I thank for your presence in my life, whether it was for "a season, a reason or a lifetime". You were someone with whom I journeyed into outer space in my search, unbeknownst to me, for those stars that would light up my life to live vibrantly. You are all part of why I am who I am.

If your name does not appear on those pages, and you know it should, please know that I either ran out of pages or memory (most likely the latter) but know that you dwell in my heart. Add your name to your own book if you have one and let me know so that I can add your name to my personal copy. As a matter of fact, if you feel so inclined and deserve a mention, please let me know and I will send you a book, with my personal addition of your name! I am serious!

THE T AFFIRMATIONS PAGE

Repeat those that you wish to apply to you today

In all my pursuits I practice great TENACITY. I press on TENACIOUSLY, failing forward if I must until my goal is reached.

I TREASURE those in my family TRIBE and look for positive traits to emulate.
I am loved and accepted by my family TRIBE for who I am and all that I am.
I accept my TRIBE members for their uniqueness and all that they are.
I keep open honest relationships with my TRIBE.

I use TENDERNESS to show gentle affection and concern for loved ones.

I attract like minded people to my TEAM of friends.
I invite vibrant people into my TEAM circle of friends.

I engage in friendship, affection, connectedness and camaraderie to create TOGETHERNESS and belonging in my community.

To be TRUE to myself, I forgive my imperfections and I forgive those who have wronged me. I practice releasing and letting go.

I TREAT myself with respect and kindness.

I am thankful for my tribe, my teams, and the tender and together moments with all those who have entered and enriched my life and my world.

CHAPTER 9
Life is Like a Box of Analogies

Forrest Gump, the lead character in the movie *Forrest Gump* (1994), played by Tom Hanks, uttered what became an often famously repeated line:

"My mom always said life was like a box of chocolates. You never know what you're gonna get."

I have a number of analogies to which I have uniquely compared living life and maintaining its vibrance. I have fun creating these and here I share with you a few of my favourite "Vivianisms".

Life Choices are Like Intersections
The Game of Life Played Out on a Four Lane City Street

I do a lot of thinking when I'm on the road driving. You know that inner voice that doesn't stop talking? The one that keeps you company when you are in the shower, cooking, trying to get to sleep, while in an elevator, while doing daily routines. My non-stop best creative thoughts come to me while driving alone. Even so, I have not been in any accident as a result of these conversations with myself!

Our life decisions can lead us to encounter many green lights that help us roar forward towards our goals, our destinations, our dreams. Whether it's a simple "right decision" to wear the appropriate outfit to an event, or a more difficult one that affects the long term success of a business, if it works, just like that satisfaction of whizzing by others as we drive through the green light, we revel in those successes. The green lights bring us closer to our goals and wow how we love those advanced lights! We are grateful for those opportunities when we shine. We feel good. We feel accomplished. We congratulate ourselves. Yes! It feels good.

Then there is reality. Reality throws us different curve balls. There are many unforeseen factors in life just as there are at busy intersections. Let's dissect this:

The amber lights slow us down or beckon us to be cautious and think a bit more before running the light. The red lights stop us completely. These are the times when we get frustrated, discouraged, angry, turned off, distracted. Even the most difficult experiences bring wisdom.

The other day coming home from visiting my youngest grandchildren, 30 minutes southwest of my home, my inner voice was very actively vibrating thoughts and ideas. I had chosen the more direct route: a straight 4-lane city road running south to north and then east to my destination.

It may not have been the fastest route, certainly not the one the app WAZE would have chosen, especially since there were so many lights along the way, but it was the route in which I thought I had the least decisions to make…the straight and narrow, or so I thought!

As I was approaching the first of many red lights to come, I realized how the journey home was like life in general. A far stretch of the imagination? Not really!

At the first intersection, I had a choice to make. Do I stay in the left lane, where a car may choose to suddenly turn left at the traffic light and delay my green light opportunity? With oncoming

Life is Like a Box of Analogies

left turners, and no advanced turn light, the journey will be further delayed by the number of cars in the oncoming lanes. If left turners are only able to do so at the amber light, it might mean my journey is delayed even more by yet another red light. The alternative: Do I make a quick move into the right lane, where I might be hindered by who knows how many cars that decide to turn right, slowing down drivers behind them? What might make this even slower would be pedestrians crossing that road, causing those turning right to wait even longer to actually make their turn.

And just like that, I realized my journey to my destination was like life itself.

In life there are many choices and decisions to make. In many cases you are not presented with enough information to help you make the choice and you have to go with your gut. It's a risk. It's an unknown. And you rely on your best instincts to help you through the moment. You rely on what experience has taught you. Sometimes it's just good old guess work.

For my first red light encounter, I chose to stay in the left lane. I could tell that oncoming traffic was fairly light and from what I could tell there did not seem to be any left turn signals blinking. That was all I had to go on. I was basing my decision on common sense. However, as life tends to give us unexpected surprises, so do intersections. There is potentially that driver who chooses to turn at the last minute. That's when frustration and anger (usually in the form of curses) erupt inside the waiting cars. I made my decision and hoped for the best as the green light indicated to me that I was able to move forward!

I congratulated myself for making the right decision as I drove by the fancy corvette in the right lane (big smile on my face). I noticed the long line of cars in the right lane, drivers unhappily waiting while two cars patiently waited for senior pedestrians to slowly make their way across the street, until they could finally turn. I was elated! I had successfully ventured forth and I gloated. Yes I did. I am not proud to say that but I did!

Prematurely I might add. The next light I approached was just turning red and the decision lay before me again. I guessed incorrectly this time, not expecting the car ahead of me to suddenly decide to turn left and, as the red Corvette whizzed past me on the right, I could feel the driver's satisfaction. I had to wait through two red lights. I'm sure you've all been there. I didn't catch up to the corvette until 3 lights later after making some different brilliant decisions.

Sometimes, just as in life, you must just go with the flow. The lane you were in was the one you were meant to be in. If it caused you to be a few minutes later, so what? Sing along with your radio, listen to the audio, plan your meal, think of how grateful you are. So many thoughts can calm the mind rather than trying to race with an anxious mind to the finish line.

We are always making decisions. That inner voice stage director talks to the person we are at the moment. Are we going to be bold? Is this something that needs to be fast tracked? Are we in a rush to get there? Is there a deadline? Perhaps this journey is simply one where we can go with the flow, one where we can relax, go with what is and what's meant to be, whatever light is in front of us. Every destination goal is different.

Some decisions are easy when we have all the facts and details in front of us. And even then, we sometimes make poor choices. Those choices set us up with a learning opportunity for the next time. We don't always know the outcome. Some successes happen by pure chance, pure luck. Some happiness occurs by the law of attraction.

And other successes happen by living a vibrant life no matter what and paying it forward.

You are the driver of your journey. How fast or slow you go depends on you. The Vibrant Life is lived by one who stops when they need to, yet passionately, albeit sometimes cautiously, moves forward with courage and conviction to reach their destination.

When you reach your goal and look back at all the difficulties you had, you will realize that it was just a process that you had to go through to make it worthwhile. If your destination was home, you got there, didn't you?

In the meantime, through your travels encountering blinking lights, red lights, amber lights, green lights, advanced lights, travel vibrantly!

- Play the tunes on the radio that help you sing along.
- Have fun mimicking the singers, like Elvis!
- Listen to audios that help you grow, think, reflect, and breathe.
- Have pleasant conversations with your passengers and get them off their cell phones.
- Stay light. Laugh.
- Look around. Take in the sights, the delights. Even construction zones are interesting, especially if you have children in the car.

Life is Like a Light Bulb

Light Bulbs & Life Bulbs

A light bulb on its own will not emit brightness. It needs a source of energy and a switch to help direct its shine. Take ceiling lights or potlights for instance. When we flick the appropriate switch, suddenly a dull, dark room can light up with vibrance.

Life is our light bulb, in fact our "life" bulb. We can keep it dim and lifeless or we can ensure it has an energy source and manipulate the switches in such a way as to turn on our energy full blast! For those occasions where we wish to be low key, a listener, an observer, we can use a dimmer to dim the light to help others shine. When we want to present our power, our verve, our vitality, our vivacity, it is only a matter of moving the dimmer up all the way. The choice is always ours.

When you switch on your light, your life bulb, is the energy of aliveness coming through you? Have you sparked your inner energy and allowed your passion to rise? Our core energy is our vibrance! Energy gives you empowerment to live life at a high frequency. Energy is the vibration. You simply need to switch it on and ensure its energy source.

Life bulbs, like light bulbs, can burn out. Light bulbs are easily replaced and reset in that lamp which allows us to see more clearly, to appreciate what is really in that darkened room. We are fortunate to have many tools to help us when our own life bulbs burn out from mental or physical exhaustion or whatever happenstance. Unlike the light bulb, easily bought on Amazon or in the neighborhood hardware store, life bulbs are reignited by choices you individually make to first find your own energy sources. Through reciting affirmations, expressing gratitude, receiving life coaching, meditation, yoga, exercise, reading, or even conversations with a trustworthy friend, you can help the life bulb that needs replacing. You can switch it on and be a spark of inspiration to others by turning up your own light! Vibrance begets vibrance!

Life is Like Water in Nature*

Travel Through Life as Water Through Rocks

Picture water in its many forms and think of your own self.
Do you flow like water?
Are you rigid like ice?
Are you hot and bubbling?
Or are you feeling stagnant and sludgy?
Whichever you most resonate with today,
you can be sure that just as water changes and adapts constantly,
so will you.

Water is the centerpiece of all life. As we strive for a happier, more vibrant or fulfilled life, we can take our inspiration from water. Often it's necessary to adjust and adapt just like water working itself downstream despite the obstacles it may meet, like logs and rocks in the river.

The way in which water navigates obstacles can inspire us to work similarly with our own challenges. Water will not force its way through an obstacle. It will effortlessly find another way to get around it.

Have you ever had the experience where you had to make a change in order to navigate obstacles and make things flow? Have you taken online classes in order to practice yoga, or did you have to learn to work from home, do all your shopping online, or the million other things that changed in the past two years as we found ourselves needing to go with the flow during the great upheaval of COVID?

We have to be adaptable, receptive to the possibility of change and willing to make the change, or we become rigid and stagnant. Change is necessary in order to find peace of mind and go with the flow. This is the water element. It's about adaptability and it's a good thing we have it!

Take a nature walk to an area with a small stream, river, lake, ocean or even a big puddle. Watch the way of the water and think of new paths you might pursue to assist you to float through the waves to reach your goals and live your dreams. There is a vibrancy to the way water moves. Observe! Go with the flow!

*idea thanks to my yoga mentor and healer Gisele Mogan

Life is Like a Sunset
(…but not what you think!)

There was a time when I would be terribly upset to see scattered clouds forming at dusk ruining what I thought would be the perfect sunset. In reality, after experiencing more than my share of magnificent sunsets from our cottage dock, I noticed that the more the mix of clouds appeared among patches of clear skies, the better the overall sunset's long lasting magical effect.

I believe all of us want life to resemble the perfect sunset we usually long for. We wish life to be disturbed by nothing but a clear path to follow with little interference or challenges.

Have you noticed though that when the sun sets through a clear blue cloudless sky, the orange beauty on its clear descent usually dissipates once below the horizon? Done! Fini! At the same time, there is no doubt in anyone's mind that a golden sunset is one of nature's striking beauties!

When there are hazy clouds with scattered interference in the otherwise blue sky, especially near the horizon and just above, the golden ball leaves our world with much more brilliance and vibrancy and a much longer lasting after effect. After breathing in the sunset, I spend at least a half an hour marvelling at the palette of pinks, oranges, mauves and violets in the darkening night sky. Long after the sun has said goodbye, streams of colours are shared in the Western sky as if to reward us for a hard day's work!

While we wish life were easy, it will never be so. Every night will not offer a clear sky for Mr. Sun! We are grateful for perfectly clear days, yet the reality is that every day will not offer that clear undisturbed day for us either. A life of cloudy skies, one with challenges, difficulties and hurdles, invites us to be more active, on purpose, more animated in our approach to obstacles, stronger to jump over. How else do we become great problem solvers and learn from the lessons life provides through experience? How else do we learn to bounce back?

If we compare life's passage to that of a sunset, we know we too can have a greater long lasting brilliance and ultimately impact all those who look to us for advice, for nurturing, for care and for love. We can model how to flow through intermittent clouds. We can show others how to re-enter the path of clarity with deeper strength and commitment. We can awaken to a new day more beautifully, energetically, vibrantly, and remarkably.

The ups and downs of life are meant to build character so we can emerge as glorious and stunning as a sun setting into a cloud scattered sky.

GO VIBRANT!

> *I was walking along, minding my business*
> *When love came and hit me in the eye*
> *Flash Bam Alakazam*
> *Out of an orange coloured, purple striped*
> *Pretty green polka dot sky*
> *Flash bam alakazam and goodbye*
> - Milton Delugg/William Stein, "Orange Coloured Sky"

Life is Like a Roller Coaster

We have all heard this expression so while we are on the topic of ups and downs, let's explore this often heard statement: "My life is like a roller coaster!" This is often muttered by someone who is frustrated with the trials and tribulations of their busy hectic life. Here is a new thought for you: If your life is indeed like a roller coaster, congratulations!

The fact that you even decided to go on this life journey means that you have shown up brave, courageous and willing to pursue its unknown turns and twists. Your life is vibrant! It's full of excitement. Roller coasters are for the adventurous as is life itself. Who wants a life that is dull and boring? There will be times in life, as on those steel monsters of amusement parks, that your heart will beat like never before, you will scream for joy, you will close your eyes in fear, you will celebrate getting through scary moments, you will overcome turbulence. There may be a steep dip but you will climb to new heights and, no matter what, you will survive! Just breathe!

People will line up, waiting for hours upon hours to get a chance to ride the beast, queasy stomach and all, just to be exhilarated for three or four minutes! And they will say it was all worth it! Sometimes you have to wait for life to present to you that which was meant to be yours. With the right positive attitude, taking in the lows with the highs, you can experience all the wonderful things life has to offer. It's up to you! VIBRANT You! And when you do so with trust, you will undoubtedly say that your life journey, much like a roller coaster, was well worth it!

HEY VIBRANT YOU! IT'S YOUR TURN.
Create your Own Analogy!

Let your vibrant mind take over with your own creative version of what "Living a Vibrant Life" reminds you of.

Here are some starters for you. Think of some quickie ideas that would give credence to the idea and then skip to writing your very own idea with a full out explanation!

Again, we could bundle these together and store them in a book (or a box…with chocolates!)

ANALOGY STARTER IDEA 1
LIFE IS LIKE A GARDEN

_____
_____
_____
_____
_____
_____

GO VIBRANT!

ANALOGY STARTER IDEA 2
LIFE IS LIKE A GAME

_____
_____
_____
_____
_____
_____

ANALOGY STARTER IDEA 3
LIFE IS LIKE A TREE

_____
_____
_____
_____
_____
_____

ANALOGY STARTER IDEA 4
LIFE IS LIKE A RAIN SHOWER OR A BATHROOM SHOWER

_____
_____
_____
_____
_____
_____

YOUR OWN VIBRANT IDEA 5

LIFE IS LIKE....................................

CHAPTER 10
Not The End

There are so many other things that I learned from my journals that I wish I could put into this book, my labour of love. I have so thoroughly enjoyed my journey through the various VIBRANT stars, on my "out of this world" experience, through my JOURNAL universe into the VIBRANT Galaxy and am immensely sad that it seems to have arrived at its last destination.

I leave you, my dear readers, with a treasured note I found in one of my journals from 2016, which I would have missed, had I not ventured on this journey. This note was intended to be written by me as an "older person". This was an exercise planned for our Arbonne team at a retreat organized by my business partner Amanda and myself. We were all to think of a year in the future where we would be writing back to the person in the present (that being Vivian of August 2016) to thank them for what they had accomplished in the years to the future you, so that you could live the life you were living on the date you chose. I chose to write to myself on my 77th birthday, November 20th, 2022, just because I liked the lay of the numbers. I had forgotten all about it until now. I opened it a tad early but with divine purpose. I didn't even remember the contents. I was touched and emotional. Here it is!

Dear Vivian of 2016, (from Vivian of 2022)

I am writing this to you on November 20, 2022 and I am presently 77 years old. It is my birthday and though I am surrounded by many friends and family, you are here with me too. I want to tell you how appreciative I am of all you have done for me to bring me to this place of joy. As I sit here in my villa in Portugal, waiting for the school year to be over so that my grandchildren can visit their "Vava" and "Pop" (not all at once of course), I realize that it's because of you; it's because of who you are and who you were, why I am here today.

Thank you for continuing to have that joy of life, that joy of living, joy of newness and the openness to try new things that actually brought me here, in this special place of contentment, with no worries of money or time. Thank you for your persistence in pursuing a business so foreign to you but that you were willing to at least try.

Thank you for looking after your body, mind and spirit. I am so grateful for your attempts to stay healthy and live a life of good health as even now at 77 I am still as healthy as all get-out. Thank you for making "Health and Wellness" such a priority for you. You watched what you ate, ensuring that your body had the proper nutrients to avoid old age diseases. And good for you that you kept up with yoga, cardio classes, weights, walking, water aerobics and dancing to help me be in the shape I am in. Rowland continues to tell me that I look better than many 40 year olds. Now I wouldn't be entirely truthful if I did not admit that I still can down a full bag of Lays Regular Potato Chips without even thinking twice!

Not The End

I want to especially thank you, Vivian 2016, for being so much fun, so vibrant so positive and spreading that, not only to your own life, but to others. People still think I am younger than I am and still ask me how I get my energy! I have you to thank for getting me into a very good skin and nutrition routine. And I am trying my best to remember to drink lots of water!

There were some things you decided to stop as it was no longer empowering you but in fact sabotaging you. Thank you for loving and releasing. Thank you for letting go of your frustrations with yourself and with others. Yes you are a person that has high expectations of yourself and all your family members. I know it was hard for you to try your best to sometimes ease off and I am sure you had to keep reminding yourself often. I especially know that you let yourself be disappointed by others. I want you to know it was totally okay that you sometimes failed to understand that you weren't always able to be in control. At least you became more aware of the truth and the reality as being part of the necessary journey to where you wanted to go and now you are here where I am. You are more understanding now and you let things go more easily. Truth be known, this is still something I need to strive for.

Thank you Vivian for starting to give others in this world the gift you believe would help others live their dreams. And look at whom you have changed? I am so proud of your accomplishments. We have touched so many lives, both of youth and of adults. We have so many friends from all over the world, some young and some old like me, who have become fabulous friends who exude positivity and a belief in themselves.

The fact that you were open to suggestions that were made to you about some balances you needed to achieve in your life and the fact that you listened to ways to make you an even better person and leader, helped me be more calm at 77. So while my family might disagree with that,

I truly am not as obsessed with perfection in myself and others. I still strive for it, mind you, for as you know, you can't remove all the spots from a leopard.

I love the way you cared for and established such amazing relationships with your grandchildren. They all love their Pop and Vava. I am hoping that at my age we have maybe one or two more and would love another girl. The joy of seeing my grandchildren growing up makes me realize everyone has a unique personality and we have to love everyone where they are at. Their different personalities make each one so delightfully different and fun.

I want you to know life is good. In fact, life is wonderful. Life is a blessing. I try to live it as vibrantly as I possibly can. I love and am loved and I have you to thank!

Loving you with all my soul and heart to the moon and back,
Your older self,
Xox Vivian of 2022 (aka Viva, Vava)

✳✳✳

DO YOU KNOW WHAT YOU ARE?

Do you know what you are?
You are a manuscript
of a divine letter,
You are a mirror
reflecting a noble face.
This universe is
not outside of you.
Look inside yourself;
Everything that you want,
You are already that.

-Rumi

Not The End

I am so grateful for my youth, my past, my age, the many lessons I have learned, the challenges I have had, the sadness, the grief, the pain, the joys, the laughter, the tribulations, the silliness, the downfalls, some of the shit I have endured, the highs I have experienced and all the aspects of just plain living life itself. Everything I have encountered has helped me become a better person ready to face what the world still has in store for me. And I know I still have lots to learn.

I know I am not perfect. I know that even with over 70 years of experience, I will still make mistakes but I promise to forgive myself for those times to come. I look forward to continuing to live life to its fullest and I say: "Bring it on! I am ready for it!" Because I do VIBRANT well!

*"I hope that in this year to come, you make mistakes because
if you are making mistakes,
then you are making new things,
trying new things,
learning, living,
changing yourself,
changing your world."*

-Neil Gaiman

Go Vibrant!

HEY VIBRANT YOU! IT'S YOUR TURN.
I'm Gonna Sit Right Down and Write Myself a Letter

Your task:

Find a lovely piece of writing paper and a letter sized envelope. Copy what is below:

FROM: Your NAME and a future YEAR (perhaps choose a "you" that is 5 years older?)
TO: Your NAME and present year

Content:

What are you going to say to thank your past self for being who you are a few years from now?
What did you accomplish in the years in between?
What did you let go of that was not serving you well?
How did you continue to grow?
In what areas did you expand?
How did your activities help your future?
How are you going to show your gratitude to your past self?
Jot some of your ideas and notes here:

_____
_____
_____
_____

continue on next page

Ideas and notes cont.

_____
_____
_____
_____
_____
_____
_____
_____
_____

Now write it on your special paper! Write it from the heart. Address it. Seal it. Put it in a location where you know you will find it in the future!

And guess what I am going to do now?

For me, it is not the end of my journey nor do I hope it is for you. I plan to have many more adventures, take many more paths and explore many more of life's avenues that will fuel my desire to continue to live life with curiosity, vibrancy, and a joie de ME!

And so…

I am going to write a letter from myself five years from now, at the age of 82, written on November 20, 2027 to my now 2022 self because this is definitely…NOT THE END!

****

LIGHT UP YOUR LIFE

Just when you thought it was over, I encourage you to take on this one last task.

LIGHT UP! For each ingredient in the Viva Vibrancy Formula, evaluate yourself as:
3 = I definitely do that already
2 = I can see myself tackling this aspect of vibrancy and am willing to try
1 = This is way out of my comfort zone and thus I will come back to this, maybe?

Star One: Viva La Vs

- ☐ Be a VISIONARY
- ☐ Find your unique VIBE
- ☐ Practice VISUALIZATION
- ☐ Create your VIBRATION
- ☐ Know your VALUES
- ☐ Live your VALUES
- ☐ Add VALUE to others

Star Two: Inviting the I's

- ☐ Invite your I AM
- ☐ IMAGINE
- ☐ Have INTERESTS
- ☐ Be INTERESTED
- ☐ Be INTERESTING
- ☐ Set INTENTIONS
- ☐ Be INSPIRED
- ☐ Be INSPIRING
- ☐ Live with INTEGRITY

Star Three: So B it!

- ☐ Be BOLD
- ☐ Be (you)
- ☐ Be BRAVE
- ☐ BELIEVE
- ☐ Be BODACIOUS
- ☐ Be a BADASS

Star Four: Roar those Rs

- ☐ ROAR your being
- ☐ RECHARGE your energy
- ☐ Engage in ROUTINES and RITUALS
- ☐ Show RESILIENCE
- ☐ Radiate RADIANCE
- ☐ REFLECT on Self
- ☐ Use ROSE-COLOURED GLASSES

Star Five: Ace the As

- ☐ Take ACTION
- ☐ Be ADVENTUROUS
- ☐ Seek ACHIEVEMENTS
- ☐ Live AUDACIOUSLY
- ☐ Create ABUNDANCE
- ☐ Have an ATTITUDE of GRATITUDE

GO VIBRANT!

Star Six: Start with the N Game in Mind

- ☐ NURTURE Yourself
- ☐ NOURISH Yourself
- ☐ Learn to say NO
- ☐ Be one with NATURE
- ☐ Find your NIRVANA
- ☐ Be NAUGHTY
- ☐ Be NICE
- ☐ Be a tad NUTS

Star Seven: Fits You to a T

- ☐ Be a TENACIOUS TRAILBLAZER
- ☐ Get your vibe from your TRIBE
- ☐ Try TENDERNESS
- ☐ Select your TEAM to compliment you
- ☐ Choose TOGETHERNESS
- ☐ Be TRUE to forgiveness
- ☐ Be THANKFUL

What's your score?
Do it again 6 months from now.
Score an even higher vibration!
Viv xox

Heartfelt Acknowledgements & Gratitudes

*Feeling gratitude and not expressing it
is like wrapping a present and not giving it.*
-William Arthur Ward

I am truly grateful to my incredible family members both biological and blended, some who have passed, yet all who were, are and continue to be the most important people in the world to me.

THANK YOU FOR BEING IN MY LIFE...

Omi & Opi: Marie & Jack Ader,
Mom & Dad: Ursula & John Leinung;
In Laws: Nathan & Helen Shapiro, Helen James
Rowland Dunning
Jody Shapiro, Kaori Noguchi, Alejandro Olivares, Noriko Noguchi
Todd Shapiro, Irina Shapiro, Sawyer Shapiro, Scarlette Shapiro
Karen Connort, Fred Timman, Laurenn Connort, Michael Schecter, Sahara Schecter, Lev Schecter, Jude Schecter, Justin David, Nadine Halligan, Norah David
Julie Dunning, Dan Lundberg, Camryn Fitzgerald, Lindsay Fitzgerald, Reed Fitzgerald, Anna Lundberg, Chris Dunning, Carla Dunning, Georgia Dunning, Max Dunning, Joe Dunning, Isabelle Dunning, Sarah Green, Alex Green, Ella Green, Charlie Green

Go Vibrant!

Herbert & Ursel August, Manuela August, Pedro Singer, Miguel Blaufuks, Constança Urbano de Sousa, Dani Blaufuks, Miri Sonnenfeld Blaufuks, Max Sonnenfeld Blaufuks, Laura Ebert, Charlotte & Sophie

My life is more magical thanks to the many friends, business associates, acquaintances & pets who have graced, influenced, inspired, and/or touched my life! There are many!
I am grateful for you…

THANK YOU FOR BEING IN MY LIFE…

Aaron & Anika Guthrie, Abby Kubik, Addie Van Gessel, Adriana Tesler, Ailish Keating, Alden Howell, Aldis Stefansson, Aleksandra Jurevich, Alex Trimble, Ali Goldenberg, Alicia Graham O'Brien, Alija Tandecka. Allison Carr, Amanda Fingerhut, Amy Powers, Amy Sky, Analyse Gonzalez, Andi Jones, Andrea Grace, Andrew Gibson, Andree Nottage, Andrew Rose, Andy Alexander, Aneesha Jacko, Angela Harders, Angela Zekkou, Anna Cyzon, Anna Liotta, Anna Mintz, Anna Miyata, Anne Hochkirchen, Anouk Flambert, Anthony Lue, Ariel Gerard, Aunt Betty, Avi Gordon, Barbara Goldenberg, Barbara Howard, Barbara Majeski, Bella Luna, Bernard Winterton, Bernice Eisenstein, Bernice Carnegie, Bernie Little, Bettina Braj, Bev Little, Bev Panikkar, Bill Clendinning, Bill Givens, Bill Taub, Billie Short, Bob Loewenthal, Bob Peter, Bobby Kountz, Bonnie Dennis, Bounce, Brendon Samuels, Bret Mitchell, Brian Goldenberg, Brianna Greenspoon, Brittany Krystantos, Bruce Howell, Bryce Harper, Camilla Scott Eves, Carl Goldenberg, Carla Lupo, Carly Immitt, Carole Borgh, Carolyn MacDonell, Catherine McMillan, Cathy McBey, Cele Pasternak, Chona Navarro, Chris Comeau, Chris

Heartfelt Acknowledgements & Gratitudes

Green, Christy Dreiling, Cinzia Cavalieri, Claire Risoli, Clare Forshaw, Claudia Ortiz, Colleen Petersen, Connie Drapeau Kennedy, Corinne Sklar, Corvette Morris-Barclay, Courtney Kelly, Cynthia Ehrlich, Daisy Kulick, Dale Koshida, Dana Shalit, Danielle Larice, Dave Bradley, Dave MacNeill, David "Flash" Moscoe, David Baird, David McBey, Dawn Richard, DeAndra Harmony, Deborah Wilson, Denise Germaine, Desiree Lindeque, Destiny, Diana McBey, Diane Bovalino, Diane Dalton, Diane Taub, Diane Westcott, Dianne Leggatt, Dick Allen, Dilaila Longo, Divya Shivcharan, DJ Kaminsky, Dominique Drouin, Dominique Hendred, Don Sklar, Donna Weiser Hennes, Doris Kaminsky, Dorry Korn, Doug Trimble, Douglas Bird, Dr. Hope, Dr. Joseph Leventhal, Drs. Lubberddink and Luby, Dylan Dreiling, Eddie Keystone, Edona Caku, Eileen Oliver, Elaine Broadley, Elaine Pardi, Elana Samuels, Eleanor Winter, Eli Javitz, Eli Rubenstein, Emily Leitner Brown, Emmy Alcorn, Enzo Lib, Eric Spitz, Erica Lieberman-Garrett, Erin O'Brien, Eronica Aljoe, Errol Lee, Eugenie Choi, Eva Kessel, Eva-Marie Tropper, Evlynne Braithwaite Householder, Elyssa Kirsh, Fay Kruzel, Fern Stimpson, Fionna Blair, Frank Colaiacovo, Fred Grise, Gail James, Gavin Herman, Gena Lowe, Giancarlo Quaglieri, Gilda Niman, Gilda Spitz, Gillian Weinrib, Gina MacMillan, Ginette Guimond, Gisele Gordon, Gisele Mogan, Glen Conduit, Glen Tobin, Gloria Clamen, Glynis Gilman, Goldie Hawn, Gordon Fraser, Greg Clarke, Greg Prince, Harold Stone, Heather Skoll, Helen Eidlitz, Helen Graham, Helena Alexandre, Helena DeBruyn, Herbert H Carnegie, Hilde Herman, Hope Cruz Clark, Ian Hamilton, Ian Leventhal, Ilana Orrelle Meltzer, Inge Spitz, Iris Kavanagh, Jack Muskat, Jack Prince, Jackie Williamson, Jake Disman, Jan Westcott, Janice Bell, Janice Martell, Janice Mitchell, Jasma Thomson, Jay Keystone, Jay Sobel, Jayon Anthony, Jean Michel Bargoin, Jeff Goldenberg, Jeffrey Peter

Wyndowe, Jen Jackson Calafiore, Jena Alma, Jenn Bugden, Jenn Johnson Poirier, Jennifer Mercier, Jerry Roisentul, Jerry Wiesenfeld, Jerry Zeit, Jessica Baker, Jessica Eckler, Jessica Levy, Jessica Louise Beal, Jessica Stephens, Jessica Thomas, Jessica Welch, Jill Farren, Jill Kahn, Jill Kay, Jill Savage, Jim Ainsley, Jim Sgueo, Jim Strachan, Joel Clamen, Jo'el Douglas, Joel Shapiro, Joanne Foote Levy, JoAnne Lanktree, Jody Weintraub, Joe Nakkar, Joey Ing, Johanne Messner, Johanne Pelletier, John Alcorn, John Alcorn, John McCullough, John McLean, Johnnie Williams, Jon Waisberg, Jordana Leventhal Vermaat, Joseph Rubenstein, Josh Eckler, Joy Bryan, Judith Siegel, Judy Gelman, Judy Mack, Julia Knight, Julie Danaylov, Julie Martell, Juliette Trudeau, Kalyna Bobyk, Karen Arlis, Karen Calmon Lukeman, Karen Clouter, Karen Colquhoun, Karen Cryer, Karen Donaldson, Karen Hand, Karen Hoffman, Karen Jarvis Adams, Karen Sgueo, Karen Waller, Karim Mirshahi, Kat Sanfor Creary, Katherine Bruni O'Neil, Kathleen O'Brien, Kathy Van Luit, Katie Bock, Katie Carey, Katische Haberfield, Kayla Harris, Ken Saul, Keri Kubik, Kerk Murray, Kerry Burrows, Kia Condorousis, Kim Bourne MacGregor, Kim Carmella Swartz, Kim Parry, Kimberley Neater, Kimberly Sunshine Parry, Klaus Reif, Krista Imrie, Kristen Martelli, Kristine McPeak, Kruti Patel, Ky Lee Hanson, Laine Tiro, Lalita Patel, Lara Donsky, Laura Muirhead, Lauren Gallidoro, Leigh Anne Saxe, Leona Curtis, Leslie Oland, Lesley Rubinoff, Lidia Kuleshnyk, Linda Blum Huntington, Linda Pasquino, Linda Ray, Linda Sciberas, Linda Stone, Linda Tobin, Lindsaya Van Deusen, Lisa Alexander, Lisa Beth Tomey, Lisa Gelman, Lisa Phillips, Lisa Rueff, Lital Mintz Snir, Lori Payton, Lorne Ordel, Lorrie Herman, Lorry Pasternak, Louise Squires, Lowell Dennis, Luca Vitali, Ly Raha, Lydia McGregor, Lyn Vrensen, Lynda Pogue, Lynn Walding, Lynne Gabriel, Lynne Talbot Clarke, Maddie Prince, Maggie Green, Marg Boyd, Margaret

Heartfelt Acknowledgements & Gratitudes

Peter, Marguerite Jackson, Marguerite Macdonell, Mariana Thomas, Marianne McElroy, Marianne Patterson Hendrix, Marianne Stinson, Marianne Zin, Marilyn Caplin, Marion Davidson, Marion Goldmintz, Marion Joyce, Marilyn Caplin, Marilyn Novack, Mark de Hart, Marla Gold, Marla Pancer, Marlene Allen, Marni Angus, Marta Pozniakowski, Mary Catherine O'Brien, Mary Jo Rodgers Boyd, Marion Goldmintz, Marion Joyce, Matthew Levy, Maura McGroarty, Maureen Rose, Max Albin, Maxine Lieberman, Mel Margolese, Melanie Lieberman Jackson, Melanie Marcus, Melinda Schmidt, Melodee Findlay, Michael Collymore, Michael Fagan, Michael Kelly, Michael Nissenthal, Michael O'Brien, Michael O'Brien (2), Michael Rutherford, Michel Brisson, Michelle Mikolis, Michelle Phillips, Michelle Shafir, Mike Arlis, Mike Dubois, Mike O'Brien, Mina Love, Mindy Grossman, Miriam David, Miriam Pearlman, Mitch Kyrstantos, Mitzi, Munira Cassim-Pierre, Myra Albin, Nada Youwakim, Nadine Harper, Nancy Evanoff, Nancy Greenstone, Nancy Kroner, Natalie Leventhal-Vermatt, Natalie Zombeck, Neil Williamson, Nero, Nick Condorousis, Nicole Doray, Nina Hillier, Nynke Kramer, Oedile Daniels, Pamela Lavorgna Terrigno, Patricia Yeatman, Patti Delany, Patti Durkee, Paul Fitzgerald, Paul Forte, Paul Graham, Paula Anstett, Paula Seigel, Pedro Singer, Peggy Bourne, Peggy MacNeill, Pene Gerber, Peter Chubb, Peter Nixon, Peter Skillen, Peter Spitz, Phil Penney, Philip Cachia, Phyllis Margolese, Polly Brothers, Rachel Sklar, Raisy Ordel, Raquel Jones, Reema Rafay, Reena Sheres, Reesa Quilliam, Renee Hays, Renee Leventhal, Rey Carr, Rhea Edwards, Rhonda Grace, Rhonda Matias, Richard Little, Richard Paul Geer, Richard Samuels, Risa Alt, Rita Leventhal, Rob Brown, Rob Fraser, Rob Kruzel, Robbi Condorousis, Robyn Posen, Rochelle Carnegie, Ross Meltzer, Russell Payton, Ruthie Baumal, Sally Roberts, Sally Suen, Sam Youngz,

Samarps, Sammi Dreiling, Sara Wonacutt, Sarah Alter, Sarah Brigid Brown, Sarah Hate, Sarah Wade, Sharon Attias, Sharon Basman, Sharon Buckler, Sharon English, Sharon Wiesenfeld, Sheila Kempke Greene, Shelley Blackburn, Shelley Thompson Robbins, Shirley Stanton, Shivani Patel, Shonnie Grise, Skid Crease, Solveig Berg, Sondra Sullivan, Sonia Kurney, Sonia Vitali, Sophie Kubik, Stacey Brass-Russell, Stan Caplin, Stella Loy, Stephanie McNamara, Stephen Feldman, Steve Macdonell, Steve Poirier, Steve Schmidt, Steve Winter, Suchita Sanjay, Sue Brown, Sue McNeil, Sue Shirin Cassidy, Sue Zimmerman, Susan O'Connor, Susan Phillips, Susan Saxe, Susie Singer Sereda, Sweetie Frankel, Sylvan Valleyway very new Condo friends, (*you know who you are!*), Sylvia Farbstein, Tabatha DeBruyn, Tage Singh, Tammy & Rita Cohen, Tanya Escoffery, Ted English, Teea Aarnio, Terry Goldenberg, Terry Samuels, Thomas McBey, Tina Koch, Tom Kubik, Traci Lynn, Tracy Manley, Tracy May, Val Darien, Vera Ing, Verna Campbell, Veronica Lacey, Vic Wonacutt, Vicki Poitier, Vivek Patel, Vivian Singh, Vivian Tesler, Vivien Bonnist Cord, Wayne MacDougall, Wendy O'Neill, Wendy Bouwman, Wendy Lukonen, William Rabbitts, Yuri, Yvonne DuBois, Yvonne Georgopulos, Zanele Njapha, Zed Condorousis, Zizi El Ghatit, Zoe Porter

"Gratitude and love are my tools in navigating my human experience"
Zizi
Remembering: A Spiritual Journey A Guide
by Zeinab el Ghati

READ MORE!

So pleased to participate with 19 additional authors in the Amazon International Best Seller, ENTANGLED NO MORE, orchestrated by the brilliant Katie Carey!

"Entangled no More"
Co Author Vivian Shapiro

You can order the kindle or paperback version of this Amazon International Best Selling book, in which I am a co-author!

5.0 out of 5 stars Amazon Review (Verified Purchase)
Reviewed in Canada on September 17, 2022
A Courageous account of moving from Discord to Harmony

I was especially moved by contributing author Vivian Shapiro. She offers an intimate portrayal of her courageous movement from a traumatic, discordant relationship in her life to self-fulfilment and harmony. Her struggles have joyfully resulted in a free and vibrant life, one which inspires others.

ABOUT THE AUTHOR

Vivian Shapiro is an energetic, positive-minded influencer, grateful to be active and vibrant at 75+ years! Recently, she became an Amazon International Best Selling Author for her contribution to the multi authored book *Entangled No More*. She is a writer of music, children's books, plays, poetry, retirement party and conference scripts, as well as a singer, actor, dancer, choreographer and more.

As a Toronto teacher, vice principal and principal, and later Education Director of a charity for youth, she spearheaded programs and conferences to empower disenfranchised young people. She is a recipient of the 2012 *"Amazing Aces in Action Award"*, and the 2018 *"Celebrating Outstanding Women Award for Philanthropy"* both for her work with the Herbert H. Carnegie Future Aces Foundation and the community.

As a mom to a blended family, she loves engaging as "vava" to her thirteen grandchildren. As Regional Vice President with Arbonne International, she coaches and trains people to create a life of choice and abundance. Vivian has a passion to help others defy aging by immersing themselves in a healthy lifestyle no matter gender or age. She sees herself as the shining light to help be the spark for others.

AFTERWORD

Thank you dear reader! I hope you found this book enjoyable and that it made you laugh, cry and think. My hope is that this book did have some meaning for you and helped you in any way, shape or form.

*And if you loved this book,
I would like to ask you
to "give back" in the form of a review.*

Every review matters, and it matters a *lot!*
Head over to Amazon or wherever you purchased this book
to leave an honest review for me.
I appreciate the time you take to do this and thank you endlessly!

Manufactured by Amazon.ca
Bolton, ON